the chicken

❧ HANDBOOK ❧

A Practical Guide to Keeping Hens
and Other Fine-Feathered Friends

the
chicken

❖ HANDBOOK ❖

A Practical Guide to Keeping Hens
and Other Fine-Feathered Friends

Vivian Head

FOX CHAPEL
PUBLISHING

First Published in the United Kingdom by Arcturus Publishing Limited, 2010.
First published in North America in 2012, revised, by Fox Chapel Publishing, 1970 Broad Street,
East Petersburg, PA 17520.

ISBN 978-1-56523-686-8

Library of Congress Cataloging-in-Publication Data

Head, Vivian.
  The chicken handbook / Vivian Head.
     p. cm.
Includes index.
ISBN 978-1-56523-686-8
1. Chickens. I. Title.
SF487.H4177 2011
636.5--dc23
                          2011024127

To learn more about the other great books from Fox Chapel Publishing,
or to find a retailer near you, call toll-free 800-457-9112 or visit us at **www.FoxChapelPublishing.com**.

Note to Authors: We are always looking for talented authors to write new books. Please send a brief letter describing your idea to Acquisition Editor, 1970 Broad Street, East Petersburg, PA 17520.

Printed in China
First printing

CONTENTS

INTRODUCTION

There is nothing to beat the sound of contented poultry as they go about their daily life in your garden. There is also nothing better than eating eggs straight from the nest, knowing the birds that laid them weren't cooped up in some shed for 24 hours a day.

The majority of us love our dogs and cats, and they don't even give us anything back except loyalty and affection. Poultry, on the other hand, do. Once you have sat down to freshly laid eggs for breakfast, you will never again be tempted to reach for that carton on the supermarket shelf. Home-laid eggs are full of flavor because they have not been sitting around for days, or even weeks, waiting for delivery. There is even a difference in the color of the yolks—a healthy orange instead of that washed-out yellow we are used to. Unlike other pets, poultry do not need to be walked, brushed or fed twice a day. Essentially, all the poultry keeper needs to do is gather the eggs daily, fill the birds' food and water containers, and change their bedding about once a month. It couldn't be easier.

If you take the plunge you will be able to impress your friends and family with truly organic produce. All it will take is a few birds and some organic feed. Research suggests poultry allowed to roam free with access to grass, lay eggs that are higher in Omega-3 fatty acids and Vitamin E, while also being lower in cholesterol than any sold in retail stores. These are much healthier for you and are very beneficial to your skin and hair.

Chickens are the easiest poultry to start with. You might think, particularly if you have never been around chickens, that they do not have much of a personality. That is where you would be mistaken. They are quite unique in their own quirky way, and love nothing better than to be in the company of humans. You can indulge them with special treats and, if handled from a chick, are quite happy to be held and petted. They come in so many different varieties that you will find it hard to choose just one.

Poultry are fascinating to watch and have really interesting habits, such as dust bathing. This is where they dig themselves a shallow pit in sand or dry soil and wriggle around in it to get the dust between their feathers to keep their plumage free of mites. They love to sunbathe, so don't worry if you see them relaxing on your lawn with outstretched wings, they are just taking advantage of the sun's warmth. By raising chickens, you will be taking one more step toward sustainable living. Think of all of the packaging you will save by not buying eggs or chicken from the supermarket. They will also help to eat your unwanted leftovers and their feces can help give you a nitrogen-rich compost heap. Eggshells are a great addition, too, especially where there is a lot of chalk in the soil.

Left to roam free in your garden, chickens will get a lot of their own nutrients from a variety of sources including grass, worms, snails, ants and other insects.

Chickens will happily live with other birds such as ducks and geese, and they are a cheap and rewarding hobby. Remember, though, they can live to a ripe old age of 15, so they are going to be around for a long time if you don't intend them for your dinner table. They will probably lay for about four to five years, before their laying capabilities begin declining.

If, after reading this book, you decide you would like to take up keeping chickens as a hobby, please bear in mind they are escape artists. They seem to have an uncanny knack of finding any weakness in fences. They will also need to be locked up at night to keep them safe from predators, but they will always go back to their coop as soon as they sense dusk, so catching them is not normally a problem. They need natural daylight to produce eggs, so make sure you let them out as soon as possible in the morning.

Finally, despite their many merits, keeping chickens in your back garden is still relatively uncommon. So now is the time to amaze your family and friends by picking up your favorite chicken and cuddling it. They will probably be shocked to see it fall asleep in your arms as you tenderly stroke its comb and wattles. Also imagine their surprise when you show them bright green eggs from your Ameraucana hens.

Here are just a few simple tips to think about before you take up your new hobby:

• Find a bird vet before buying any birds.

• Make sure you know someone who will happily "birdsit" for you when you want to go away from your home for more than a day.

• Read a book on keeping chickens.

• Make your neighbors a prime consideration so keep the area your chickens live in as clean as possible.

• Check on local rules and regulations regarding livestock.

• Consider very carefully before buying a rooster, as the noise and trouble they create is usually not worth it.

THE HISTORY OF CHICKENS

Most of us, when we think of chickens, envisage the farmer's wife taking out her kitchen scraps to a few hens pecking around the yard. The remainder of their time was spent foraging and scratching in the dirt to supplement their diet. They probably didn't lay many eggs, but they were certainly contented birds—far removed from the battery hens now bred to cope with modern-day demands.

The domestic chicken has evolved from the Red Jungle Fowl (*Gallus gallus*) of southern and southeastern Asia. These jungle fowl lived in flocks, which had a dominant male and a definite social pecking order. Our domestic chickens have many things in common with their distant relatives, who spent their time scratching round their indigenous habitats searching for food. At night they would seek shelter in the forests or when danger threatened. They have little natural oil in their plumage, so chickens try to stay out of the rain as much as possible because their feathers cannot readily shed rainwater.

There is controversy regarding when domesticated chickens first reached the Americas with evidence suggesting them being brought through the Polynesian Islands to Chile around 1350 A.D., and other evidence suggesting they were brought by the Spanish conquistadors. Most modern day breeds found in North America can trace their roots to Europe, although great leaps forward in breed development occurred in the United States in the twentieth century. The original farm hens were dual purpose, being bred for both their laying and meat qualities. Gradually, through selective breeding, these characteristics were developed separately. Lighter breeds were produced for their egg laying, and bigger, heavier breeds for meat.

Little by little other breeds were introduced from Europe and the East. Some of the best breeds were produced in North America around the turn of the twentieth century, perhaps the most notable being the Rhode Island Red and the Leghorn.

After World War I, many ex-servicemen started their own poultry farms as the demand for fresh food increased. These were always free-range and it was quite common to see large fields filled with grazing hens. As demand increased, more intensive methods of raising poultry were developed. In the 1950s and 1960s, the preferred method was deep-litter, where many hens were housed together indoors on bedding of straw or shavings.

This progressed in the late 1960s and 1970s to the system we have today—intensive battery farming. This is where hens spend their lives—one laying season—in tiny cages without foraging for their own food or experiencing any daylight.

For centuries, cock fighting was one of the main reasons for keeping poultry.

In recent years there has been a lot of negative reaction toward this method of keeping chickens, and we are again seeing a resurgence of part-time farmers and smallholders who keep chickens for their eggs, meat, and their own pleasure. More consumers may some day prefer free-range over the desire to buy cheap poultry.

DID YOU KNOW?

- The chicken was the first domestic animal to be mentioned in recorded history. It is referred to in ancient Chinese documents as the "creature of the west."

- Romans considered chickens to be sacred to Mars—their god of war—and built chicken cairns (mounds of stones in the shape of a chicken) to worship him.

- The Gauls considered the rooster as a symbol of courage.

- In Christian religious art, the crowing cock symbolized the resurrection of Christ.

- Buddhists believe the first enlightened animal was the Tibetan chick of Chidarti.

- The Trobriand Chicken People from Papua New Guinea are one of the first human societies to be based on the chicken.

- The rooster was the emblem of the first French Republic.

- The Wild Man of Rhode Island was the first man to pluck a live chicken in order to tar and feather another man.

- One punishment for an adulterous wife in medieval France was to make her chase a chicken through town naked.

- It is illegal to eat chicken with a fork in Gainesville, Georgia.

WHAT IS FREE-RANGE?

In the past "free-range" was a general description, meaning that poultry were allowed to roam at will over the fields and pastures. It was once very popular with farmers who would allow the birds to graze on the stubble after they had harvested their crops. The birds obtained much of their food this way, as well as ridding the fields of insect pests and unwanted weed seeds. A hen house was always provided for shelter and as the grazing became exhausted and it was time to move on to a new field, the house would be moved with them.

This system was very popular because for most of the year, the birds found their own food, which meant that feeding costs were greatly reduced. They helped build up the fertility of the soil, especially where other livestock were grazed, because their pecking and scratching would help spread the nutrients from their own and the livestock's droppings. There were disadvantages, of course—losses of birds to foxes and other predators were high. Also eggs were often laid in hidden nests and frequently got missed when it came to collecting. Finally, cold winters killed off many hens, meaning egg production could dwindle to virtually nothing.

Today, free-range means much the same as it always did, although poultry usually has its space in a garden, an orchard, or a smaller field. To be labeled and sold commercially as "Free-Range" in the United States, the producer must provide proof to the U.S. Department of Agriculture that the chickens had access to the outdoors and were not confined to a pen. The requirement covers meat, but not eggs, which are often labeled as "Cage-Free" instead of or in addition to "Free-Range."

In other countries, the labeling requirements for "Free-Range" can be more restrictive, covering the design of hen houses, the number of birds allowed based on the amount of space available, and the number of hours birds have access to open air.

SO YOU WANT TO KEEP CHICKENS

Probably, like a lot of people, you are concerned about the amount of chemicals that go into food these days, especially if you have young children. More and more people have started to grow their own vegetables, so the next logical step seems to be to keep two or three hens in your back garden. You will soon learn it is surprisingly easy and very pleasurable as well. It is becoming increasingly popular, probably because hens make such charismatic and endearing family pets. It is a hobby your children can easily become involved in, especially when they can get their hands dirty mixing together the food from household leftovers. You can also be safe in the knowledge that hens are not unhygienic. On the contrary, chickens will spend hours just cleaning themselves.

As you get to know your chickens, you will soon discover each one has an individual personality or characteristic. At the end of a hectic day, there is nothing more relaxing than to stand and watch your chickens strutting around the garden, fending for themselves.

Before you go out and buy your first hens, you will need to be aware that you must devote a certain amount of time each day into looking after them, just as you would with a dog or cat.

You will need to consider where you are going to keep them, whether you have a friendly neighbor who will feed them when you are away, and how secure the site is against predators, even in the city.

Local zoning, land use, and other regulations vary and should be consulted before you determine if you can pursue a backyard flock of chickens and what size your flock will be. Above a certain number will likely be classified as a commercial venture. At the beginner stage, two or three hens would be adequate to get you started and allow you to determine if raising poultry is really the hobby for you.

Your neighbors will be another consideration, because there is no point in causing unnecessary upset if they are adamant they do not want to live next door to any livestock. You can probably win them round though, when you tell them that chickens don't smell and that they will actually eat slugs and other pests from the garden. Provided you don't buy a rooster— which often are banned by zoning regulations—that will no doubt wake them and you up at the crack of dawn, a few bantams running round the back garden shouldn't cause any problems at all. You can always keep neighbors sweet by giving them a carton of fresh eggs each week, as well.

Your hens will soon pay for themselves. If, say, you have three hens, you can expect them to lay as many as 600 eggs a year— they will be large, extremely fresh, and would have cost far more to buy. You can determine the savings yourself by checking the cost of eggs in your local supermarket.

Thanks to the current trend for keeping poultry, there are now complete starter kits including housing, feed, and the hens themselves. So if you are still keen there is nothing to stop you.

KEEPING URBAN HENS

Keeping hens in urban areas is becoming increasingly popular, but requires a slightly different approach than in rural areas. At the outset, it is advisable to check that you are allowed to do so. Even if you are a homeowner, the use of your property for livestock may not be allowed. There may also be regulations governing the location and construction of a coop, as well as the number of birds allowed.

If you are a renter, each landlord will have his or her own rules on the matter, so you will need to check your rental agreement carefully.

Wherever you live, you will need to demonstrate at all times that you are taking the utmost care of your hens' welfare. Change bedding and clean runs regularly and dispose of any waste products sensibly.

Because space will be more of an issue in an urban setting than in a rural one, you might like to consider one of the smaller breeds of chicken—many come in bantam size, which are approximately a quarter of the size of some of the larger breeds. The

Buff Orpington (*below*) is a good choice for beginners, as are the Cochin bantams. Both breeds are great layers, nice natured, and make excellent pets. If you are in any doubt as to what breed to buy, you can always visit a fellow urban dweller who keeps chickens and seek their advice.

Beginners always ask how much space a chicken requires. The rule of thumb is to allow 4 square feet inside the coop for each chicken and 10 square feet outside. Always allow your chickens to roam freely if you can, provided you have a safely fenced-off yard or garden. Hens usually like to stay fairly close to their coop, and as long as you provide them with regular food and water, they shouldn't look to wander.

Because roosters can be noisy, it is not advisable to keep them if you have neighbors close by. You might also like to check online for any local vegetation that could be toxic because chickens love to eat greenery. Should you find any, either dig it up or fence it off.

THINGS TO CONSIDER

In the initial excitement of receiving your new hens, you might overlook a few important points, so it is a good idea to check the following:

SECURITY

Have you made sure your garden or yard is completely secure? This is very important because hens can behave like those birds in the movie *Chicken Run*! Not only should the area be designed to keep your chickens in, but it should be secure enough to keep people and predators out. It is a good idea to try to keep your hen house out of sight—the less attention you draw to it the better. Not only will this ensure your hens are less of a nuisance to your neighbors, but it will keep prying eyes away from your precious stock. Unfortunately, vandalism is a concern today, so taking these simple precautions makes sense. Laying a shingle path down the side of your chicken run will also help alert you to unwelcome visitors.

CONDITIONS

Hens love bright and airy conditions, but you will need to make sure the hen house is sheltered from strong winds and driving rain, and has some shade for the hotter summer days. You need to make sure your hens have perches to sleep on at night. Ideally these should be placed higher than the nest boxes so that the chickens are not encouraged to sleep in them. Also, if you have more than one perch they need to be designed in such a way that the chickens are not directly below each other. Finally, the perches should be easy to remove for cleaning. Remember, your hen house needs to provide fresh air without drafts, as stale air can cause health problems. Ventilation is usually provided by a window, roof ridge or ventilation holes covered with galvanized wire mesh.

TIMBER

Has the timber on your hen house been treated so that it can withstand the weather? If you are treating the timber yourself, you must make sure it is completely dry before introducing your hens, because they could be adversely affected by vapors emitted by the treatment material. You also need to make sure that the roof is completely watertight and insulated to provide extra protection during bad weather.

GRASS

Hens love to peck around the ground eating insects and worms, but you have to remember they will also defecate on the grass. This can quickly become a muddy mess, which is not pleasant if you have young children or other pets. If you only have a small area of grass, then it is probably best to keep your hens within a specially prepared run. It is a good idea to dig out the base of the run and line it with a pond liner. On top of this you can put any number of substrates—woodchip, compost, soil, or even some turf. After a few weeks when its benefits have been exhausted by the hens, it can be removed and composted.

PREDATORS

A chicken, with monocular vision (eyes on either side of its head) sees many things as a predator; even a passing plane can be a problem to them. They require the security of cover, otherwise they will not have the confidence to go out and forage for themselves. This harks back to the chicken's jungle origins. Trees, hedges, and sides of buildings are ideal, and provide shelters high enough off the ground to allow them to duck underneath when feeling threatened.

The main enemy of the free-range chicken, both urban and rural, is undoubtedly the raccoon. He is particularly a problem during autumn and winter when other sources of food are becoming scarce. A raccoon will generally hunt at night, starting its hunt as it becomes dusk. In winter, however, raccoons may start a lot earlier, while it is still light, which means before your chickens have been put away for the night. Once they have located hens, raccoons will return again and again, so you need to keep an eye out for signs of intrusion. If you challenge a raccoon on a nightly basis by scaring him off, it will eventually give up, so it pays to be vigilant. Make sure your run is protected by a good stiff mesh capable of withstanding an animal the size of a raccoon, and that the mesh is buried at least a foot under the ground. Also make sure any joins are overlapped and securely wired together.

Rats can also be a major pest. It is very difficult to totally exclude rats from chicken runs and houses, so regular control to keep numbers down is essential. Rats are particularly dangerous because they carry Weil's disease, a condition that is potentially lethal in man and transmitted through rat urine. Rats can also carry pasteurella and salmonella, so making sure they cannot get into a run or hen house is a major concern. If you are placing poison, you need to make sure it is completely inaccessible to chickens, wild birds, domestic pets and, of course, children. Rats will not attack an adult bird, but are adept at killing chicks and breaking into eggs.

There are an increasing number of birds of prey, particularly sparrowhawks, inhabiting city areas. Although they will not take on a full-size chicken, the smaller bantams are much easier prey. Trees make their task harder, and a run with a mesh roof is also very important.

Anatomy of a Chicken

A SIMPLE CREATURE

Unlike other mammals, birds are relatively simple creatures. Although you do not need to know everything about the anatomy of a chicken, most beginners like to learn as much as they can before embarking on their new hobby.

The diagram on the opposite page is designed to help you identify any parts of the chicken's anatomy that are mentioned in the book. There are a number of organs that are unique to birds, and some interesting features, too, such as the mechanism designed to take the place of teeth. Because they cannot grind up food like a mammal, the hen has to break down the food in other ways, which are discussed in detail on page 20. The hen's gut is very basic in design, so it is important that you keep to a suitable diet, especially if you know it is one that suits their digestive system. Hopefully by learning all the different parts of their anatomy, you will be able to quickly identify when something goes wrong.

The chicken's immune system is also extremely simple, and relies entirely on the gut to provide it with all the nutrients it needs to fight off disease. When the gut is impaired, either by incorrect feeding or by a parasitic infection, a hen can get very sick. Chickens seem to be able to withstand bad weather and mite infestation, but anything beyond that and their immune system starts to break down.

EXTERNAL ORGANS
Combs

All chickens have combs on the top of their heads, but they do not always look the same. The comb is a fleshy growth, in both the male and female and, depending on the breed, will vary in size, shape and color. The majority of combs are red; some breeds have purple combs. This feature is not just there to make the bird look pretty. Combs play a very important role in controlling body temperature, helping the chicken to cool down; chickens do not sweat, so they rely on other methods to cool down.

In the case of the female chicken, the comb also shows the cockerel when she is ready to mate; the comb flushes with blood. It also acts as a guideline to other females when they are determining their pecking order.

There are eight distinctive types of comb on chickens and roosters and we're going to examine each in turn:

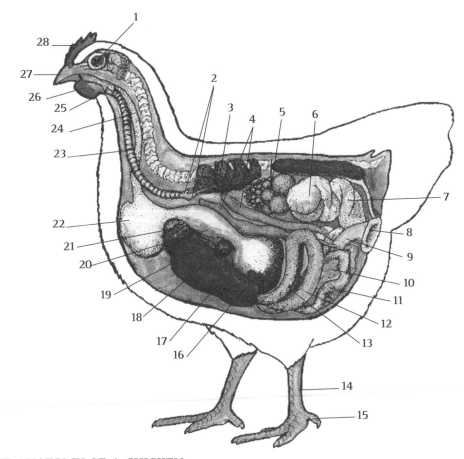

THE ANATOMY OF A CHICKEN

1. Eye
2. Bronchial tubes
3. Lungs
4. Ceca
5. Ovary
6. Kidney
7. Oviduct
8. Cloaca
9. Large intestine
10. Mesentery
11. Small intestine
12. Duodenal loop

13. Pancreas
14. Shank
15. Toe
16. Gizzard
17. Liver
18. Spleen
19. Gall bladder
20. Proventriculus
21. Heart
22. Crop
23. Trachea
24. Esophagus

25. Superior larynx
26. Wattle
27. Beak
28. Comb

The rose—is a solid, broad and nearly flat comb on top. Low and fleshy the comb ends in a well-developed tapering spike at the back. In the Hamburg breeds it can turn upward, or in the Leghorn it is nearly horizontal. The top surface of the main part should be slightly convex and studded with small, round protuberances.

The strawberry—is a low comb positioned toward the front of the head. The shape and surface resemble the outer part of half a strawberry, hence its name, with the large end closest to the beak.

The silkis—is an almost round, somewhat lumpy comb, which is usually greater in width than length. It is covered with small corrugations on top and crossed with a narrow, transverse indentation slightly to the front of the comb. Some have two or three small points toward the rear, which are often hidden by a crest, while others have none.

The single—is a moderately thin, fleshy formation with a smooth, soft surface texture. It is firmly attached along the top of the skull from the beak. The top portion shows five or six deep grooves or distinct points, which are higher at the middle. The comb is always upright and much larger and thicker in males than in females.

The cushion—is a solid, low, moderately small comb with no spikes. It is smooth on the top and the front, and the rear and sides are nearly straight with rounded corners.

The buttercup—resembles a crown and consists of a single leader from the base of the beak. It is set firmly on the center of the skull and is completely surmounted by a circle of regular points.

The pea—is a medium-length, low comb, the top of which is marked with three low, lengthwise ridges. The center ridge is slightly higher than the others. The outer ridges are either undulated or marked with small rounded serrations. This is a breed characteristic found in Brahmas, Buckeyes, Cornish, Cubalayas, and Sumatras.

The V-shape—this comb is formed of two well-defined horn-like sections that are joined at their base. This is a breed characteristic found in Houdans, Polish, Crevecoeurs, LeFleche, and Sultans.

Wattles

Both male and female chickens have distinctive wattles. This is a fleshy piece of hanging skin just underneath their beak and combs. These organs, together with the combs, help to keep the bird cool by redirecting bloodflow to the skin. In males, the combs are often more prominent, though this is not the case in all varieties.

Eyes

The eyes are positioned on the side of the head. They focus not by changing the shape of the lens, but by changing the shape of the cornea, taking advantage of any forward vision they can achieve. Their eyes have a greater acuity than those of humans, which means when you stand close to them, they can see your clothing in great detail. Their three-dimensional vision is poor, which is why they tend to bob their heads up and down to get a more accurate idea of the depth of objects by changing their focus. The eyelid, which is called the nictitating membrane, moves horizontally across the eyeball and is normally translucent. This must be kept moist, so you have to ensure your birds always have enough water to wash their faces periodically in spells of hot weather.

Beaks

In the absence of teeth, the beak plays an important role in feeding. The serrated edges of the beak contain nerves that enable the chicken to sense exactly how hard it is biting. This is very important when hens are handling a chick, allowing them to ascertain exactly how much pressure they are using so as not to damage the young.

Ears

Chickens have ears—more like ear holes—just below and behind the eye. They do not possess an outer ear, or pinna, as most

mammals possess, but do have ear lobes. A chicken's hearing is acute. Apart from lice, chickens rarely have ear problems.

Hackle, saddle and breast

The hackle is where the breast meets the neck. Sometimes these feathers are raised at times of aggression, hence the saying 'getting your hackles up!' The area directly behind this is called the saddle. The breast is toward the front and at the center of the body and is disguised by the flight feathers.

Wings

The power in the chicken's wings comes from its breast muscles. Chickens do not fly any distance but will use their wings to gain height for roosting, or getting over the top of a fence if they really want to escape.

Wing bars

These are the brighter feathers on the wing, which cover the flight feathers.

Feathers

It is the feathers at the end of the wings (primary flights) that provide the chicken with the most thrust. They are the longest feathers on the wing. The secondary feathers are behind these and provide some lift. Many farmers use the practice of clipping (cutting the end off) the primary and secondary feathers on one wing to prevent the bird from flying.

Legs

The upper part of the leg, or thigh, is hidden by the fluffy feathers that cover the lower half of the animal. The lowest knuckle, at the hock, is where the feathers end and the shank—which is covered in scales—begins. At the back of the leg below the hock is a protruberance called the spur, which is barely visible in some breeds. The claws at the bottom have opposing toes, which are designed for gripping. These claws are worked by the leg muscle and the movement of the leg as a whole is powered by a large group of muscles equivalent to the hip and buttock muscles in humans.

INTERNAL ORGANS

The digestive system

The chicken has no teeth and consequently the food is swallowed whole after being picked up by the pecking action of the beak. Because of the beak's serrated edges, the chicken is able to tear off pieces of food such as the tips of grass, but there is no biting or chewing action to break down the food before swallowing.

Once the food is swallowed it passes down the gullet into the crop, which acts as a temporary storage pouch. If you handle a chicken shortly after it has eaten, you can still feel the grains of corn in the crop.

While the food is in the crop, it is moistened and softened by the secretions from the mouth, gullet and crop, making it ready for digestion. From here it continues its journey downward into the proventriculus. This is where the gastric juices containing hydrochloric acid and the enzyme pepsin start to break the food down. From there it passes into the gizzard.

The gizzard is a type of bag that has extremely strong muscular walls that contract and relax. The gizzard also contains small particles of grit, or tiny stones, that the bird has swallowed to aid digestion. These grind up the food, and it is in the gizzard that the hard work of breaking down the food takes place.

After the gizzard, the food passes into the small intestine, via the duodenum. This is where the enzymes from the liver, gall bladder, and pancreas take over the work the gizzard started. Bile from the liver is temporarily stored in the gall bladder, then moves in to emulsify fats in the partially digested food matter. This allows the enzymes to complete their digestion.

Once the food has been broken down into separate constituents, it can be absorbed by the blood capillaries called villi, which line the wall of the small intestine. From here, the blood carries it to every part of the body where, in conjunction with oxygen carried from the lungs, it provides the necessary nutrients for the chicken's survival.

Any particles that have not been absorbed by the blood, pass from the small intestine into the large intestine. Because chickens do not have a bladder, they do not urinate. The kidney filters the urine which then passes into the latter part of the large intestine via ureter tubes. Projections called caeca reabsorb some of the water, but the waste urine and feces are both expelled from the cloaca. The whitish part of the bird's droppings is the urine.

Breathing

The chicken has a pair of small lungs situated inside a ribcage consisting of seven pairs of ribs. They have no diaphragm, so the lungs are attached to an interconnecting series of air sacs. These sacs act just like bellows to ventilate the lungs. The lungs also have another function—thermoregulation. As chickens have no sweat glands, heat must be lost through the respiratory tract by panting. Panting birds need to be put in the shade, as too much heat can cause problems. The nerves that control thermoregulation are situated in the neck; as they pant the area can be cooled well below the body temperature, which can cause sunstroke.

Cloaca

The word cloaca quite literally means sewer, and it is the area into which both the oviduct and the intestine empty. Female birds are able to turn part of the cloaca and the last segment of the oviduct inside out (just like a glove). This means the vent is then everted and the egg emerges far outside at the end of the bulge. As a result, the egg does not come into contact with the walls of the cloaca and does not become contaminated by the bird's feces. In addition, the intestine and inner part of the cloaca are kept shut by the emerging egg, preventing their contents leaving when the hen strains to deliver the egg. This system ensures that eggs are always clean when they are laid.

The circulatory system

The chicken has an almost identical circulatory system to that of human beings. Like mammals, chickens have a four-chambered heart—two atria and two ventricles—with complete separation of oxygenated and de-oxygenated blood. The right ventricle pumps blood to the lungs, while the left pumps blood to the remainder of the body.

Birds in general tend to have larger hearts than mammals. This is to help them cope with the high metabolic demands of flight. In chickens, the heart plays an important role in maintaining the bird's body temperature.

Liver

The liver is the largest organ in the chicken's body and also plays a vital role. It is the organ that metabolizes most of the important substances that a bird needs. The waste product of the liver is called bile, which aids in the bird's digestion.

Spleen

The spleen is located in the abdomen of the chicken, where it functions in the destruction of old red blood cells and holds a reservoir of blood. It is regarded as one of the centers of activity of the immune system, helping the bird avoid certain infections.

Kidneys

Although chickens do not have a bladder, they do have a kidney, which drains an area in the cloaca called the urodeum. The liver produces uric acid, which is removed from the blood by the kidney.

Reproductive system

The egg is formed in the mature hen by a reproductive system composed of an ovary and oviduct. Most females have two functional ovaries, but chickens and most other birds have only one ovary and one oviduct. In this oviduct, all parts of the egg, except the yolk, are formed. The major structures are:

ovary—containing immature and mature follicles. The mature follicles consist of the egg yolk and the unfertilized ovum.

infundibulum—It is here that the ovum is fertilized if the hen has been mated with a cockerel. Spermatozoa from the cockerel are stored within the infundibulum, and are capable of fertilizing ova for up to 30 days after mating.

magnum—this is where the albumin is formed.

isthmus—this is the tough outer membrane located just beneath the egg shell.

uterus—this is where the egg shell is formed.

vagina—the egg travels through the vagina into the cloaca, from which it is laid.

cloaca—this is the external opening from which the contents of the urinary tract, the feces, and the eggs leave the hen.

The hen reaches puberty and starts to produce eggs at 4 to 5 months of age, but for breeding purposes, they do not reach maturity until they have turned 6 months. The cockerel is capable of insemination at 4 to 5 months of age as well but, like the hen, it is not used for breeding until it is over 6 months old to ensure it has viable sperm.

THE ANATOMY OF THE EGG

1. Eggshell
2. Outer membrane
3. Inner membrane
4. Chalaza
5. Exterior albumen (outer thin albumen)
6. Middle albumen (inner thick albumen)
7. Vitelline membrane
8. Nucleus of pander
9. Germinal disk (blastoderm)
10. Yellow yolk
11. White yolk
12. Internal albumen
13. Chalaza
14. Air cell
15. Cuticula

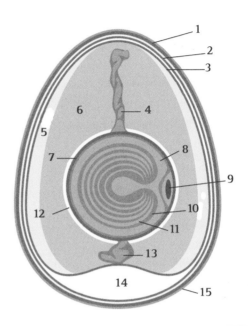

Anyone who eats eggs knows that they consist of three major parts—the shell, the white (or albumen) and the yolk; but in reality they are far more complex than that.

THE EGGSHELL

The shell is bumpy and grainy in texture and covered with as many as 170,000 microscopic pores. Eggshell is made almost entirely of calcium carbonate ($CaCO_3$) crystals. It is a semi-permeable membrane, which means that air and moisture can pass through its pores. The shell also has a thin outermost coating called the *bloom* or *cuticula*, which helps to keep out any bacteria.

A tip to keeping eggs fresh for an extra month is to dip the shell in a silica-based liquid and thus clog all the little pores.

INNER AND OUTER MEMBRANES

Lying between the eggshell and the albumen are two transparent membranes, which act as barriers against bacteria. If you give these layers a tug, you will find that they are amazingly strong. This is because they are partly made of keratin, the protein present in human hair.

AIR CELL

An air space forms when the contents of the egg cool and contract after the egg is laid. The air cell usually rests between the outer and inner membranes at the larger end of the egg, and accounts for the crater you often see at the end of a hard-boiled egg.

The air cell expands as the egg ages, so check this out when you next eat a hard-boiled egg.

ALBUMEN

The word albumen comes from the Latin word for white—*albus*. Each egg contains four alternating layers of thick and thin albumen holding water and approximately 40 different proteins.

CHALAZA

The chalaza (pl. chalazae) are opaque pieces of rope-like egg white that hold the yolk in the center of the egg. Like little anchors, they attach the yolk's outer casing to the membrane lining the eggshell. Without these supports, the yolk would hit the sides of the shell and the chick embryo would never develop. The more prominent the chalazae are, the fresher the egg.

VITELLINE MEMBRANE

This is the clear casing that envelops the yolk.

BLASTODERM

In eggs with a large amount of yolk, cell division is restricted to a superficial layer of the fertilized egg. This layer is termed the blastoderm. In birds it is a flat disc of cells at one end of the egg.

YOLK

The yolk contains less water and more protein than the egg white, a certain amount of fat and most of the vitamins and minerals of the egg. These vitamins include vitamin A and D, phosphorus, calcium, thiamine, and riboflavin. The yolk is also a source of lecithin, an effective emulsifier. Yolk color ranges from just a hint of yellow to a magnificent deep orange, but this depends on the feed and breed of hen.

Where Do I Begin?

HOUSING AND EQUIPMENT

Your first major decision will be choosing what type of housing you wish to keep your chickens in. The main criteria at this stage is the welfare of your hens and the amount of space you have available.

There are several types of chicken houses or coops to buy, but first you need to know how many chickens you are planning to keep and take it from there. If you are just starting out, then three chickens is a good number. It is not advisable to have just one, as they are social birds and need the contact of other chickens. This number allows you to keep on top of hygiene and limits the amount of scratching damage to your garden or run. Also the space needed around them changes drastically as you increase the numbers; it is not sufficient to simply multiply the ground space with the number of chickens, you need to at least double it for every chicken over two. The more space you can give a chicken, the happier it will be.

Now let's consider the type of house you would like to use. They can range in design from a one-story unit to a multiple story unit, depending on how complicated you want it to be. There are portable houses as well as permanent ones, or of course you might decide you would like to build your own.

THE CHICKEN TRACTOR

This method utilizes a fold unit, or a house complete with its own run built into it. This unit can be moved from place to place as

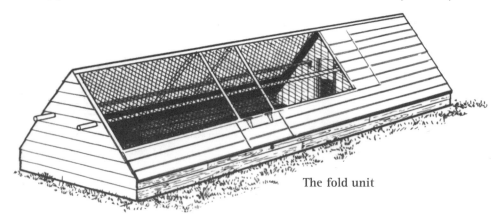

The fold unit

26

the grazing becomes exhausted, so that the hens always have access to fresh grass. It can be carried quite easily by two people, by poles that extrude from either end. The advantages of this method are that grazing is controlled and there is no build up of droppings with the consequent parasites and disease. The hens are also safer from predators.

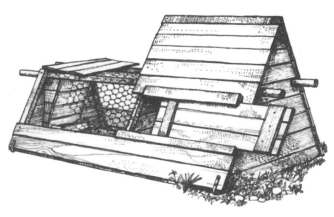

The traditional ark

RUSTIC STYLE

These are generally wooden chicken houses with overlapped boards. They are very dry, well ventilated, have a pitched roof, and are well designed for easy egg collection. The only downside is they are very heavy and the most expensive to buy. Having said that, chickens live very happily in this style of house.

ECONOMY RANGE

These are usually box-shaped and made from panels of wood or rain-proofed chipboard, with a large outer wire mesh. The egg boxes are usually integral, but are easy to get to. Cleaning is usually easier than the rustic style, especially if the sides can be removed. This type of house often comes with an integrated outer cage to act as a chicken run. They do not allow the hens much space, but they are fine if you only want to use them to confine the birds at night.

TRADITIONAL ARK

This is made of sawn timber and weather-boarding and comes already treated with creosote. It has a night house with perches, a row of nesting boxes that are accessible from the outside by a door, and an external run. It is quite heavy but can be moved by using the handles at either end.

PLASTIC HUTS

The Eglu is the latest type of hen house to hit the market and is a little plastic hutch, or mini hen house, designed to hold two chickens. It is space-age in shape and has been described as "the chicken coop for the I-Pod age." It is perfect for urban dwellers, or people with small gardens because it comes with a framed outside run and can easily be moved around.

There are many advantages to using plastic coops. They are extremely well insulated and will never need to be repaired. The other big advantage to plastic is that there are no little niches in which parasites can build up. Finally, they are exceptionally easy to clean.

Many people start off with an Eglu for two or, at most, three hens and then find that chicken keeping is an addictive hobby and they upgrade to an Eglu Cube—the larger version.

THE GARDEN SHED

Sheds are ideal places to house chickens, as long as you are prepared to give up this precious space. Garden sheds are generally easy to clean because there is plenty of room to move around, but if you choose this option you will need to pay special attention to insulation and ensure your shed is free of drafts. You might also need to reinforce the outside against predators— some types will break through the walls of a shed to get to the eggs inside.

MAKING YOUR OWN

If you have access to the internet, you will find plenty of free plans to help you build your own chicken coop. Planning is the key here. Get it right and you should end up with a well built hen house that gives your chickens enough space to live in harmony. If you are thinking about building your own, study the following checklist and

make sure you incorporate each of the points in your design.

✔ Is the coop safe from predators?
✔ Is there sufficient shade and shelter?
✔ Is there sufficient sunlight?
✔ Can the birds scratch at the soil, bark, straw, or compost?
✔ Can the birds flap their wings inside the coop?
✔ Are the birds able to reach their food without competition from other birds?
✔ Can you keep the floor of the coop dry?
✔ Can you easily reach the eggs?
✔ Is there sufficient ventilation and light?

How much space?

The actual house itself, excluding the run, should have a minimum floor area of 12" squared for each large chicken and 10" squared for each bantam. Be certain of local zoning and land use requirements before planning your coop project.

Should you decide starting from scratch is a bit daunting, there are plenty of kits on the market that come with all the materials and instructions needed to complete the job.

Regardless of the type of house you decide to use, as long as you meet your chickens' needs, you'll have contented birds laying plenty of fresh eggs.

THE INSIDE OF THE COOP

Chickens like to roost at night and you will usually see them start to congregate around the chicken house as it starts to get dark. You might find they walk in and out a few times, but eventually they will find themselves a perch and settle down for the night.

INSULATION

Wood is undoubtedly the best and warmest material for making your chicken house. Where winters are particularly harsh, you may need to provide some extra insulation. If you only intend to keep a small number of birds, they may not be able to generate enough heat to keep warm. The only problem with providing extra insulation is that you might restrict the ventilation.

The optimum temperature for a chicken is 69.8°F. At temperatures lower than this the bird will consume extra food to keep itself warm. The greatest heat loss is generally through the roof, while drafts account for about 25 percent. There are a variety of insulating materials available, including compressed, fireproof wallboard, and sheets of rigid, extruded polystyrene foam. It is a good idea to hang a thermometer somewhere in the house so you can keep a check on the temperature. In areas where it is extremely cold, another option is using an infrared lightbulb so the chickens will be in a heated environment but will not have their sleep and laying cycles disturbed. Hang the bulb where it will not create a fire hazard. Operating the bulb on a timer is an option.

VENTILATION

If a chicken is housed in a stuffy, badly ventilated coop, it will quickly lose condition and stop laying. There needs to be a continuous supply of fresh air, balanced against the need to conserve warmth. Getting the balance right is not easy, so using a thermometer is a good idea.

If you are using a large shed, then it is best ventilated by a combination of eaves and ridge ventilation. There is a gap at the apex of the roof, protected by a ridge, so that air can pass through, while rain is kept out. The air enters the side eaves, which are often protected by a baffle board. Larger houses often have windows to provide light and it is preferable to use polycarbonate as opposed to glass, as it has better insulation properties and is less likely to break.

Smaller hen houses usually have a window vent that is covered with galvanized steel mesh. This is placed high up on one wall, above the heads of the perching chickens. Other houses may have a sliding partition or window shutter to protect against bad weather. The house should always be sited so that the window is on the leeward (downwind) side.

THE FLOOR

Most of the smaller chicken houses come complete with a solid wooden floor with supports that hold it off the ground.

Most droppings will be directly beneath the perches, so it is a good idea to either have a special droppings board or a box—easily removed for cleaning—underneath. A droppings board is a section of wood that slides out easily. An alternative could be a strong piece of polythene sheeting.

Some houses come with a slatted floor, usually with 1 1/4" wide wooden or plastic slats placed 1" apart, enabling droppings to fall through to the ground below, leaving the floor in the house clean. This is ideal because when you move the house to a new site, the droppings can be easily cleared. An alternative option is to use a wooden-framed floor with a mesh panel. The slatted floor, however, may not be adequate for winter-time use. In a cold area, you'll want to cover it with solid flooring.

You may choose to use a coop with an absorbent layer on the floor—pine sawdust makes an excellent material for this as the oils in the pine give the hut a pleasant aroma. Alternative materials include bark, wood chippings, and straw. Straw is particularly good because it adds to the insulation of the coop. If you are keeping your hens in an urban situation, then it is advisable to change this type of bedding once a month. It is compostable, so disposing of it should not be a problem.

PERCHES

Every house should come with at least one or two perches, depending on the number of birds for which it was designed. The perch needs to be placed higher than the nest boxes so that the chickens are not encouraged to sleep in them. Common practice allows 10" to 12" of width per bird, and more is always better if there is room.

The ideal perch should be rounded off and smooth, making it a comfortable thing for the bird to grip. The width should be around 1 1/4" to 2", but can be less if you only intend keeping smaller bantams. The depth should be about the same.

Design the sockets in which the perches sit so that it is easy to lift the perches out for cleaning. This is important because it is the favorite hiding spot for the red mite, a tiny, nocturnal blood-sucking parasite.

For the larger birds, the perch should be no more than 23 1/2" above the floor. The reason for this is they could damage their feet when they jump off the perch. Small cuts or grazes on the birds' feet can lead to infections and abscesses, a condition commonly referred to as bumblefoot.

For lighter birds the distance can be greater, but it is not advisable to place them higher than 3 feet off the ground.

If you are using several perches, the distance between them should be approximately 12" to 16", depending on whether they are stepped or parallel. Stepped perches will be placed at different heights, but the bottom one should not be more than 24" above the closest surface. If you are using single perches with a droppings board, the height is normally 8" above the board.

POP-HOLES

A pop-hole is the door by which the chickens go in and out of the house, as opposed to the one used by the poultry keeper. It is designed to be opened from the outside and used to control access to a given area. If your chicken house has been designed with a raised floor, the pop-hole will need a ramp so that the birds do not have to jump down or flap their way into the coop. The simplest way of providing this

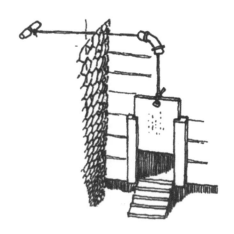

An easy way of opening a pop-hole without having to go inside the run

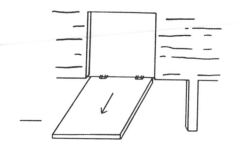

is to have a hinged door that drops down from the top and becomes the ramp (*see image*).

Alternatively, the ramp could be a permanent feature, with a door that slides up and down for opening and closing. If there is an integral run, it is useful to be able to open and close the pop-hole door

from the outside; otherwise it means you will have to keep going inside the run. You will need to make sure you can fasten the pop-hole securely at night to exclude any unwanted predators.

It is also a good idea to build some type of porch over the top of the pop-hole, as this is an effective way of keeping drafts to a minimum within the house.

NEST BOXES

If you are starting out with a small hen house, then nest boxes need to be placed lower than the perches. Try to choose the darkest area of the house, because it will encourage the chickens to go in and lay eggs and discourage egg eating. Nest boxes need to be above ground level because you do not want to encourage your chickens to lay their eggs on the floor. Ideally, the nest boxes should be accessible to the keeper from the outside of the house. The best way to do this is to have a hinged lid just above the nest boxes, making sure it is waterproof. Traditional nest boxes are around 12" wide by 12" deep by 10" high. To stop the nesting material from falling out you will need to put a panel—3 1/4" in height should be sufficient—at the base of the entrance.

Some nest boxes come with a wire mesh base, a good idea because it keeps the nest cool and helps to avoid broodiness.

If you are using free-standing nest boxes, say in a shed or barn, a section of sloping hardboard placed along the top will prevent the birds from fouling the area around them. Where a number of nest boxes are placed off the ground, there should be some alighting perches in front of them to make it easier for the birds to get in and out of them. For a small domestic hen house, allow one nest box for every three birds.

Shavings from untreated wood are one of the best nesting materials for lining boxes. They are clean, dry, free of dust, and non-toxic. Do not use shavings that have come from wood that has been treated in any way as this is toxic to the hens. They should only come from specialist suppliers.

You can use synthetic materials—for example there is a plastic material available that forms into tussocks that resemble grass. The droppings tend to drop through this material, leaving the eggs clean. It comes in rolls and can be cut to fit the size and shape of the nestbox. It is easy to clean—shake it to remove the loose droppings and then wash it in hot water.

Hens prefer material that they can push around and mold into the shape of their body. Straw is another good choice, but you need to make sure it is totally free of mites. It is not advisable to use hay, because it can become damp very quickly and mold can form. This can lead to respiratory problems in both the birds and the keeper.

DOORS

You will need a door providing access to the inside of the house. In a shed this can be a normal size door, but in a smaller coop, using a hinged section of the roof is a good idea. Your goal is reaching eggs easily, having easy access for cleaning, and insulating against drafts. Consider putting a padlock on the door—cases of theft are common, particularly of rare breeds.

LIGHTING

Providing some artificial light in winter will ensure your hens continue to lay. Do not leave the light on 24 hours a day. Chickens are extremely sensitive to the amount of daylight, so you'll want to make changes gradually if you are introducing artificial light. For example, birds accustomed to nine hours a day of daylight shouldn't be suddenly exposed to artificial light for 12 hours. It is very hard on them. Add light in no more than 30-minute increments about once per week.

OTHER EQUIPMENT

DUST BATHS

It is part of the hen's instinctive behavior to take a dust bath. This means she will be searching for an area of fine, dry earth or dust and literally wallow in it. The idea is to let the dust penetrate between her feathers and onto her skin, removing parasites such as lice, which infest the skin and the base of the feathers. Free-range hens will find their own favorite places, but if they are confined to a run, a natural dust bath may be difficult for the hens to make. It is essential, therefore, to provide one for them. A shallow, wooden box filled with fine silver sand is ideal, but you will need to make sure it is protected from rain. Fine, dry soil is also suitable, but ashes are not recommended as the alkaline conditions can lead to the spread of mites. Adding insecticide to the dust bath is a good way to help control lice and mites.

FEEDING AND DRINKING EQUIPMENT

Hens will need access to feed several times a day and to water at all times. It is, therefore, imperative to provide the right feeding and drinking equipment. If you only have two or three hens, then homemade equipment is adequate, but once you start keeping more chickens it is advisable to use manufactured feeders and drinkers. They are usually more efficient, less time-consuming and easier to clean. Food should be stored in dry, rat-proof containers. It is a good idea to have a manufactured measuring scoop as well so that you have an easy way of keeping track of the amount of food you give at any one time.

A grain grinder is another useful piece of equipment and, set at its coarsest setting it can be used to prepare grains, peas and beans. A mincer is also a good idea for use on raw vegetables, as well as a large pan for cooking up scraps and potatoes.

If you have young chicks, you can buy special feeders that allow small heads to get in to feed, but prevents the larger birds from having access.

Inside a building you can use a suspended tube-feed hopper, but it will only take dry mash or pellets. It is best to provide wet mash in a plain, open trough that allows all of the hens to have access.

If you are using a hopper outdoors, then you will need to make sure it is waterproof. If you buy a large enough one, it should be sufficient to last a weekend, if you are not around for a couple of days. There is a drawback to this, however, in that wild birds and rats might decide to help themselves.

Grit hoppers are also useful for holding limestone grit. Chickens need a supply of grit to enable them to digest food effectively. If they are free-range for much of the time they should find enough naturally, but if they are kept in a run they will benefit from an additional supply.

The most convenient way for providing water is to use an automatic one, which can be used either inside or out. You probably won't want to go to the expense of an automatic waterer if you are only intending to keep a small number of hens. The alternative is a gravity-fed drinker, which again can be used both indoors and outside, and is made of galvanized metal. It is best to suspend this a short distance above the ground or to place it on a stand, so that there is less likelihood of contamination by droppings.

Drinkers for chicks are usually made of plastic so that they are easy to keep clean. The water level can be seen through the plastic, but you will need to be a bit more vigilant with these as they can be knocked over much more easily than the metal ones.

Drinkers will need to be cleaned and filled at least once a day. In hot weather it may be necessary to do it more frequently. Five hens can drink as much as 1 quart of water a day, but this can double when the weather is exceptionally warm.

MAKING A RUN

If your manufactured hen house does not come with its own run, you will probably want to consider making one yourself. On a small scale, weather-proofed posts can be erected with galvanized poultry wire netting in between. You can also buy green, plastic coated netting, which is slightly more decorative if the run is going to be in your garden. Whatever type of netting you choose, you will need to make sure it is pegged securely into the ground, or your hens will simply escape underneath. Poultry netting also has a tendency to sag, so it will need to be strained, by pulling wire through the top and pulling it tight (see below).

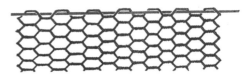

If poultry netting is used to make a run, it will need to be pulled taut by running a wire across the top.

This type of netting is not designed to keep out foxes, cats or dogs, but in a small protected garden, such predators should not be a problem as long as your birds are put away at night.

Where top protection is required, plastic anti-bird netting can be used. This is really designed for keeping wild birds out of fruit cages, but it will act as a deterrent to cats and dogs so long as it is pulled tight.

FENCING

If you are intending to keep free-range hens, then good, solid fences are a must. This is not only to keep out predators, but also to keep your chickens from wandering onto your neighbor's property.

Perimeter fencing

This is the fencing that will separate your chickens from the outside world. There is no easy or cheap way of doing this, and it is one of the most expensive jobs facing anyone who wants to keep free-range chickens. A determined fox can easily scale a fence and even if he can't leave carrying his prey, the chances are that he will already have killed several chickens anyway. A 6 1/2'-high perimeter fence of wire mesh will provide adequate protection, as long as there is a further overhang of 1 1/4" placed at an angle of 45° to the vertical. The overhang needs to be outward facing. Wire meshing with 2" holes in the mesh will deter many predators.

The bottom of the wire mesh needs to be dug well into the ground to prevent any predators from pushing their way in from underneath the fence. It is worth considering adding an electrified wire to give added security to the fence. Ideally this should be positioned 1" above the ground and 1" out from the netting. Placing another wire just above the fencing will make this barrier almost impenetrable.

Pasture control fencing

This type of fencing is only used to control the access of birds to certain areas, rather than to keep out predators. For this reason it does not need to be particularly high— 3' is usually sufficient. It should be easy to move and re-erected where required. Electrified netting is ideal for this purpose, with lightweight plastic fence posts with metal spikes that can be easily tapped into the ground. Each post should be about 10' apart. The gauge of the netting is important, with smaller holes at the bottom, increasing in size to the top. This makes sure that small chickens and young pullets do not become entangled if they touch the netting. The fence should be tensioned with straining pegs. When you wish to move the fence, the posts are simply pulled up, the net is rolled up and the fence re-erected on a new site.

ROUTINES

Before we proceed to the chickens themselves, it is a good idea to look at daily and weekly routines to make sure you will have enough time to look after your birds. People who go out to work during the day will have to time their poultry activities to the early morning and late afternoon. This is not too difficult to arrange, as long as the chickens are in a protected area that provides both shelter and shade while you are out. The feeder and drinker must be large enough to last throughout the day, and you will need to make sure they are full before you leave for work. If you are planning to be away from home, then you will need to arrange for someone to come in and feed your chickens. This does not normally pose a problem, especially if you say to the person that they can help themselves to the eggs.

DAILY ROUTINE

✔ Check that the run is closed properly, then open the pop-hole.

✔ Check that each bird is all right and not showing any signs of abnormal behavior or limps.

✔ Make sure the feeder is full and clean.

✔ Check that the drinker is clean and fill it with fresh water.

✔ Check that the hens have enough grit.

✔ Collect the eggs.

✔ Check the nest boxes and remove any soiled bedding. Replace with fresh.

✔ Give grain as a scratch feed in the afternoon.

✔ Spend some time talking to your chickens—they love human contact and will reward your attention.

✔ Check that all the birds are inside the hen house, close the pop-hole, and say goodnight.

WEEKLY ROUTINE

✔ Remove droppings board or liner and put the droppings on your compost heap. *Do not allow your chickens to have access to the compost heap.*

✔ Clean the board or replace liner.

✔ Brush out the house if necessary.

✔ Move the house and run to a new area of grass.

MONTHLY ROUTINE

✔ Worm your hens monthly by adding a preparation to their food or water.

✔ Check the house and run to make sure they do not need any repairs.

✔ Treat the birds for mites and lice if you see any evidence of them.

✔ Keep your eyes open for any unwanted guests in the feed storage area.

✔ Disinfect all surfaces once a month as part of your cleaning routine.

Choosing Your Chickens

WHICH TO CHOOSE

When choosing which breed of chicken to buy, there is a choice between purebreds, first crosses, and hybrids, as well as heavy, light, and dual-purpose. Added to these are chickens specially developed for showing, such as the utility and fancy breeds.

One of the most exciting aspects of keeping chickens as a hobby is the sheer diversity of breeds available. You have an almost limitless choice of shapes, sizes and colors to select from. However, there are many important breed-related factors to be considered when choosing your chickens. It is vital that the birds are matched to the facilities available, and that the breed temperament is suited to the environment in which they are kept.

Some chickens are bred solely for their egg-laying abilities, while others are bred for dual purposes—both for their eggs and as table meat. The most popular commercial egg-laying farms tend to use the Rhode Island Red or the Leghorn. These breeds lay white and brown eggs in reasonable numbers and are the eggs most commonly seen on supermarket shelves.

Other popular breeds include bantam chickens. Bantams are small birds, making them a very popular choice to have as pets because they are suitable for most back gardens. They are also calm in nature and relatively hardy, although the eggs they produce will be on the small size. Bantams are also used as show birds because they have many different variations of both color and feather patterns.

Let's start off this section by discussing the difference between the main classes.

HEAVY, LIGHT, AND DUAL-PURPOSE

Heavy breeds are more appropriate for the table as they are much larger and therefore produce more body flesh. They are poor fliers, easy to contain, and have a greater tendency to broodiness—the desire to sit on and incubate eggs. Because of this, they are sometimes referred to as "sitting" breeds. Examples of these are cochins and silkies.

Light breeds are smaller and have a greater tendency to fly, making them more difficult to contain. They produce more eggs than the heavy breeds and have less of a tendency to become broody. Examples of these are Leghorn, Ancona, and Welsummer.

Dual-purpose breeds have the characteristics of both the heavy and light breeds, meaning they produce plenty of meat and lay a good number of eggs.

Examples of these are Rhode Island Red, Light Sussex, and Wyandotte.

PUREBREDS, FIRST CROSSES, AND HYBRIDS

A purebred can be large or bantam-sized, and heavy, light, or dual-purpose. Purebred literally means they will always breed true. In other words, the birds will produce offspring exactly like themselves when crossed with each other, as in the Maran and the Dorking.

First crosses are birds that have been produced by crossing two different purebreds, such as a Rhode Island Red male with a Light Sussex hen.

Hybrids are the product of several different breeds. They usually demonstrate good laying characteristics in the number, size, and quality of eggs laid.

BANTAMS

Bantams started out as a genetic mutation as a result of crossing different breeds. This means the dwarf or bantam characteristics are passed on to their offspring. By the start of the nineteenth century, there were several different forms in Britain, including the Java bantam, the English dwarf and the French dwarf. Others breeds include Pekins, Nankins, Rosecombs, Sebrights and Booted bantams.

Where space is limited, bantams are a good choice, although they will not produce the numbers of eggs that, say, commercial hybrids do. The other advantage is they are very popular with children and do not require large amounts of food.

Bantam eggs are approximately half the size of normal large eggs, but this is only a generalization as it can vary on the breed, the age, and the level of feeding.

Another great attribute of bantams is they make excellent foster mothers. Many bantam breeds, particularly the Pekin, have a strong tendency toward broodiness and, for this reason, they can be used to replace stock using natural incubation.

SILKIES

The silkie (*below*) is often mistakenly referred to as a bantam because of its relatively small size. Silkies are in fact classified as "large" fowl, even though they are typically smaller than average in size. They are Asiatic in origin, have silky feathers and feathering on their legs, making them appear as if they are wearing pants.

BREEDS FOR EGG PRODUCTION

The chickens listed in this section have been genetically selected for high egg production, but usually have small bodies that make them undesirable as meat producers. Their small bodies are beneficial to egg laying because very few nutrients are wasted on building up body mass.

Egg-producing breeds are also divided up into birds that produce white or brown shelled eggs. The best white shell egg breeds are descendants of the Leghorn, with several different feather color patterns from which to choose. The best brown shell egg production breeds are developed from Rhode Island Red stock.

The color of the egg has no bearing on its taste or quality, although some people still tend to prefer to buy brown eggs where they are available, and for this reason they tend to be more expensive.

AMERAUCANA

Ameraucana is a relatively new breed that was developed in the 1970s in the United States. Ameraucanas do not have the breeding problems of their relatives, the Araucanas, and are renowned for laying eggs with blue shells. They have ear muffs and a beard and blue or slate grey legs. They are extremely hardy and sweet natured but at present are still quite rare and only available through breeders. They come in both standard and bantam sizes. The recognized varieties include Black, Blue, Blue Wheaten, Brown Red, Buff, Silver, Wheaten and White.

ANCONA

The Ancona is named after the province of Ancona in Italy and it is believed to be closely related to the original Mottled Leghorn. It was first introduced to the U.K. in 1851. Its feathers have a white V-shaped tip and a metallic green sheen. It is available in both large and bantam sizes. Anconas are excellent layers of large white shelled eggs. They are bold, active birds who make excellent foragers. The breed is available in two different varieties including the Single Combed variety and the rarer Rose Combed variety. Both varieties have white earlobes and bay-colored eyes.

ANDALUSIAN

This breed originates from the Andalucia region of Spain and is often referred to as the Blue Andalusian. Andalusians also appear in Splash (mottled) and Black. Like other Mediterranean breeds they are closely feathered, active and good layers of white eggs, sometimes producing as many as 160 eggs per year. They are relatively rare except among poultry enthusiasts and small backyard owners who are interested in preserving heritage breeds.

ARAUCANA

The Araucana was produced in South America by the interbreeding of Mediterranean breeds originally introduced by the Spanish. Originating from the province of Arauca in Chile, the Araucana is an alert and active bird with a light, long body, large and strong wings and a well developed tail, which it carries at a 45° angle. It has a quite small head with a pea comb and a face covered with thick muffling. The eggs are unique because the blue-green coloring permeates the shell rather than having a white inner layer. Araucanas are prolific layers and come in a variety of colors—Lavender, Blue, Black-red, Silver Duckwing, Golden Duckwing, Blue-red, Pyle, Crele, Spangled, Cuckoo, Black, and White.

ASTURIAN PAINTED HEN

The Asturian Painted Hen (or Pinta Asturiana) is a large bird developed originally in the Asturias region of northern Spain. It was saved from extinction in the 1980s by a few enthusiastic breeders. The most common variety seems to be black mottled with white, but it also occurs in brown, dirty white, and birchen varieties. Asturians have regular-sized crests and their ears are always red. The eyes are orange and the beak and legs are yellow with black spots. The hens lay a tinted cream-colored egg with a soft feel.

BARNEVELDER

The Barnevelder was first produced in Barneveld, Holland, just before World War I, and was imported into the U.K. about 1921. Two varieties of this bird were standardized as the Double Laced and the Partridge, with the former being the most popular today. Barnevelders are perhaps best known for their beautiful dark brown eggs. These birds are alert and upright in stature. Their wings are short and carried high, and their tails are full. They have quite small heads, a smooth face, and a single upright comb. The Barnevelder is probably one of the best choices for a garden hen because the breed is extremely docile and not easily stressed.

BRAEKEL (BRAKEL)

The Braekel is an older European breeds that dates back to 1416 and originates in the Brakel region of Belgium. There were originally two distinct types of Braekel—large and lightweight—but due to crossbreeding this distinction has vanished, resulting in one single type. The Braekel is cultivated for its egg-laying qualities; it is capable of producing up to 200 white eggs per year. A characteristic of this breed is the straight banding pattern of the feathers and the uniform, plain neck color. Several color variations exist today, with the Gold and Silver being the most common. The Braekel population declined drastically during and after World War II and is today considered to be a rare breed.

CAMPINE

The Campine is an ancient breed available in both Gold and Silver varieties. Campine chickens originated in Belgium where they have been bred for several centuries, primarily for the production of white-shelled eggs. Classed as a non-sitting fowl, the Campine is a friendly and attractive breed. Excellent foragers, Campines mature quickly and are relatively prolific layers.

EASTER EGGERS

Easter Eggers are not a true breed but a variety of chicken that lays large to extra large eggs that vary in color from blue to green to olive to aqua and sometimes a tinge of pink. The chickens themselves vary tremendously in color and conformation but are always exceptionally friendly and very hardy. This makes them ideal for a small garden and especially one with children. Beware: some breeders can mistakenly label these as Ameraucanas or Araucanas, but they are not a breed per se.

FAYOUMI

The Fayoumi is an ancient breed that originated in Fayoum, Egypt, with the primary purpose of egg production. Introduced into the U.K. in 1984 by the Domestic Fowl Trust, Fayoumis are probably not a wise choice for a small back garden. Not only are they excellent at flying, but they are escape artists as well. They scream like a banshee when captured and so would not be popular if you have neighbors close by. Technically, they are a pencilled breed rather than barred, and come in Silver and Gold.

LAKENVELDER

The Lakenvelder, with its striking black and white belted pattern, is one of the prettiest breeds of chicken. The breed has been in both Germany and the Netherlands for around 200 years, and is primarily an egg-layer. Lakenvelders are extremely active and really come into their own when kept free-range. They come in two color patterns: Black and White and Black and Gold.

LEGHORNS

The Leghorn originated in the Port of Leghorn in Italy and arrived in the U.K. in the late-1800s. Leghorns were originally white, but there is now a variety of colors available. They have white earlobes, yellow legs, and the eye is red in all colors. The females have a double-folded comb, a deep abdomen, and their legs are long and featherless. The Leghorns were one of the breeds used to create the modern battery hybrids because of their productivity and ability to adapt to all conditions. They are prolific breeders and rarely go broody. The eggs are large, white, and laid throughout the year. They are quite happy in a run, as they are free-range, but they are sprightly, alert birds that do not take well to handling. They can also be rather noisy, so possibly not a good choice for a small urban garden. They come in Black, Blue, Brown, Buff, Cuckoo, Golden Duckwing, Silver Duckwing, Exchequer, Mottled, Partridge, Pyle, and White.

MARAN

The Maran is one of the last breeds to be introduced to the U.K. It was originally produced in France in the mid-1800s as a dual-purpose breed. The most notable characteristic of this very hardy chicken is its chocolate-brown egg color. The majority of this breed is cuckoo colored, ranging from very dark grey to silver with red to bright orange eye color, with white legs. The Maran is still a popular choice with smallholders, mainly because of the egg coloring.

MINORCA

Originating in Spain, Minorca chickens can be traced back to 1780. Originally the breed was confined to the southwestern areas of the U.K. and kept specifically for egg production. However, the breed became more popular and soon it could be found all over the British Isles. The head of the Minorca is striking in appearance, with a solid red comb and white lobes. The face on both sexes is smooth and free from

feathering. Black is the main color. It is also possible to find both Blues and Whites but they are not common. The breed has been successfully miniaturized from the large fowl. The Minorca will adapt to confinement but prefers to be free-range. It is a very active and somewhat restless chicken that avoids human contact.

ORLOFF

The Orloff has never been very popular, possibly because of its strange, gloomy expression. However, it is an exceptionally hardy breed; sometimes Orloffs will lay in the winter months, which makes them very useful. It is uncertain whether they originated in Russia or Persia (Iran), but they were introduced into the U.K. in the 1920s. It adapts well to confinement, being a relatively calm bird, but does not particularly like being handled.

PENEDESENCA

The Penedesenca originated in the Spanish province of Catalonia in the first half of the twentieth century. It is noted for producing copious amounts of very dark brown eggs, said to be among the darkest of any breed of chicken. Although originally Black in color, today there are Crele, Partridge, and Wheaten colors. All members of the breed have red earlobes with a white center, red wattles and an unusual red comb. Penedesencas have a nervous demeanor that makes them an excellent choice for free-range. This nervousness subsides if the birds are handled regularly, but they prefer to avoid contact with humans and for this reason do not make good pets. They are hardy and do not mind cold winters. Penedesencas are quite rare and you might find them difficult to obtain.

SICILIAN BUTTERCUP

As the name indicates, the Sicilian Buttercup originated on the island of Sicily, more than 100 years ago. It has attracted widespread interest because of its unique beauty. The golden color and cup-shaped comb are the basis for the descriptive name. The comb is a cup-shaped crown with a complete circle of medium-sized regular points. The male plumage is a rich, brilliant orange-red with some black spangles in the feathers. The tail is a lustrous, greenish-black. The base color of the female is buff with all feathers on the body marked by parallel rows of black, elongated spangles. This gives the hen the appearance of being spotted, almost suggesting the appearance of a ringneck pheasant hen. The skin is yellow and the shanks and toes are green. The eggs are small and can be colored anywhere from white through to heavily tinted. Sicilians are good flyers and do not take well to confinement. They come in both standard and bantam sizes. However, the breed is quite rare so you might find birds difficult to track down.

SUSSEX

The Sussex is one of the oldest breeds still in existence. As the name suggests, it originated from the county of Sussex in the U.K. It is still a very popular breed to keep and will lay around 260 large eggs (cream to light brown in color) in one year. It is an alert, yet docile, breed that can adapt to any surroundings. The Sussex is an excellent forager and just as happy in confined spaces as they are free-range. The breed comes in Brown Buff, Light Red, Speckled, Silver, and White. The eyes are red in the darker varieties and orange in the lighter ones. All colors have a medium-sized single comb. The earlobes are red and the legs are white and featherless in all varieties.

WELSUMMER

The Welsummer is named after the village of Welsum in Holland. The Dutch bred this bird from the Partridge Cochin, Partridge Wyandotte and Partridge Leghorn, the Barnevelder and Rhode Island Red. The Welsummer is a placid chicken and is well suited to the small-scale, domestic environment. Rustic red and orange in color, the classic Welsummer look is epitomized by the Kellogg's Cornflakes rooster. Its eggs are dark brown and spotty. There are three variations of the standard Welsummer—Partridge, Silver Duckwing, and Gold Duckwing. There is also a bantam breed.

DUAL-PURPOSE BREEDS

A dual-purpose breed of chicken may well be an ideal starting point when thinking about keeping chickens in your back garden. Although they don't lay as well as some of the breeds mentioned on the preceding pages, they still combine the best of both worlds. The Barred Plymouth Rock, just as one example, is not only a beautiful bird, it has a lot of meat on its bones and yet still produces dozens of fine, brown eggs. Hopefully you will be able to find your "perfect" chicken among the ones listed here.

AUSTRALORP

The Australorp was developed as a utility breed from the Black Orpington in Australia in the 1920s. Primarily bred for their egg production rather than their meat, Australorps are excellent layers of tinted eggs. In the Black variety the feathers have a wonderful green sheen and this type also has a prominent dark eye. The comb is single and evenly serrated, as are their medium length wattles. The Australorp is an active breed and reaches maturity early. The birds make good pets because they are calm and friendly, although they can be a little on the heavy side for children to pick up. They will live quite happily in runs, but they do enjoy being allowed to free-range. They are not good fliers, so fencing doesn't have to be particularly high. They are very hardy and

withstand cold weather well. There are two colors—the Black, which has feathers with a lustrous green sheen; and the Blue, whose feathers are slate blue with darker lacing.

BARRED PLYMOUTH ROCKS

This heavy bird originated in the United States, and takes its name from the town of Plymouth. An historic breed, it comes with lots of pluses. Its large, brown eggs make it a suitable candidate for anyone wishing to sell their eggs. Plymouth Rocks also have yellow skin, which is the preference for those raising chickens for meat. The breed has a broad, deep and well-rounded breast and bright yellow legs. The face is red with red ear lobes, a bright yellow beak, bay colored eyes, and a single medium-sized comb. Plymouth Rocks are very friendly birds and easy to tame. They are hardy, too, and do not require a lot of space, although they still appreciate being allowed to roam free. They are not proficient flyers, and so do not require high fencing. Their tendency to broodiness means regular egg collection is important. There are several varieties of Plymouth Rock, the Barred, White and Buff being the classic ones. Other colors include Multiple Pencilled or Triple Laced, Pencilled Partridge, Multiple Pencilled Silver Partridge, Columbian, Buff Columbian, and Blue Laced.

BRAHMA

Brahmas arrived from America around the middle of the 1800s. They are sedate birds with broad, deep bodies, a full breast and long powerful, orange or brilliant yellow legs and feet that are covered with an abundance of soft feathers. The head is quite small for such a large bird, and the face is smooth and free from feathers. Brahmas have large, prominent eyes, a short beak and a triple or pea comb and small wattles. They are one of the largest breeds of chicken, and are often referred to as the "King of Chickens." They are reliable broodies, which makes them ideal if you want to raise chicks. They will happily stay confined behind fencing, but prefer dry conditions; their feathered feet can develop mud balls. Their sheer size means they are probably not suitable for someone with limited space. They are easy to tame and because they do not fly, they can be allowed to roam freely. They are also tolerant of other breeds and, unlike some

purebreds, will continue to lay eggs throughout the winter. They come in Dark, Light, White, Gold, and Buff Columbian, and in all colors the combs are red and the legs bright yellow.

BUCKEYE

The Buckeye was developed in Ohio. The plumage is a deep, lustrous red color and the legs and skin are yellow. Thanks to their pea comb, Buckeyes are cold weather hardy. While they will happily adapt to most living conditions, they do best free-range or in areas where they have plenty of room. In 2008, the breed was recognized as being critically endangered, so today is considered to be extremely rare. The Buckeye should not be confused with the Rhode Island Red, which is very similar in appearance.

CHANTECLER

The Chaltecler remains quite rare, with only about 1,000 birds in existence on small farms with an interest in preserving heritage breeds. Developed in Canada in the early 1900s by a monk named Brother Wilfrid, Chanteclers are renowned for their good egg and meat production even in the coldest of winters. They tend to be on the large side with extra-small combs and wattles, although you can find them in standard and bantam weights. They come in White and Partridge colors and they lay large brown eggs. They do not mind being confined and have a friendly, quiet nature.

CUBALAYA

Another endangered species, the Cubalaya was first developed in Cuba before being introduced to the United States in 1939. The characteristic of this breed is its unique "lobster tail"—a downward angling tail with lavish feathering. The Cubalaya comes in a variety of colors: White, Black, Black-breasted Red, Silver Duckwing, Golden Duckwing, and Blue Wheaten. The breed is slow to mature but favored because it is tame and will tolerate confinement, although males can show aggression to other cockerels. Male Cubalayas lack a spur on their legs so it is rare that any damage is caused when fighting for supremacy.

DERBYSHIRE REDCAP

The Redcap originated in the Derbyshire and Pennine district of England and is one of the oldest dual-purpose breeds. The "redcap" name comes from the bird's exceptional rose comb, which is approximately 3 1/4" long and 2 3/4" wide and is crowned with many points and an exceptionally long spike. The

birds have red earlobes. The plumage on the cockerel is deep red to black with orange neck and saddle hackles. The tail feathers are black, the legs a blueish-grey and the eyes red. Redcaps are hardy birds and not particularly broody. They are at their happiest free-ranging and are terrific foragers. They are good fliers and consequently require a lot of space. They are very good layers even into old age.

DOMINIQUE

The Dominique breed was developed from fowl introduced during the early settlement of New England. It was also the type predominating in the south of England and from which the Sussex and the Dorking descended. Dominiques are very hardy and do well on free-range as well as in confinement. They are generally calm and easy to work with. They are good mothers and reasonably good layers of light to dark brown eggs. There are both large and bantom Dominiques. In recent years there has been a revival of interest in the breed. They have black and white barring over the entire body. The rose comb is characteristic.

DORKING

This ancient breed is believed to have originated in Italy during the period of the Roman Empire, in the reign of Julius Caesar. It was introduced to the U.K. in 1845. The Dorking is

Derbyshire Redcap

exceptionally hardy and quiet in nature. These birds are active and love foraging so consequently do not do well if they are not given enough space. The eggs are a good size and white in color, with the best production occurring in the early part of the year. The breed is also prized for its white flesh and good-quality meat. Dorkings can become very broody, so regular egg collecting is important. There are five standard colors—Silver Grey, Dark, Red, Cuckoo, and White. All colors have red eyes, combs, wattles, and earlobes, with white legs and feet.

FAVEROLLES

Faverolles originate from northern France. They were created from a mix of several different breeds—Dorking, Brahma, Crevecoeur, Houdan, Coucou de Rennes, and possibly the Cochin. True dual-purpose birds, they produce a good number of eggs. Faverolles have broad, square bodies with small wings, a single upright comb, short neck, a striking beard, and muffling. The head is broad and round and the eyes are a reddish brown. The legs are tinged with pink and are sparsely feathered. Faverolles are quiet and friendly birds that tend to become very attached to their keepers. They make perfect pets for children, and will happily lay right through the winter. They are not good fliers so it is not necessary to confine them with a high fence and they will thrive whether in a run or free-range.

They can withstand the cold but they do require high-quality feed to maximize meat production. They are liable to be bullied if kept with other breeds. The breed comes in seven varieties—Black, Blue Laced, Buff, Cuckoo, Ermine, Salmon, and White.

IXWORTH

The breed first made its appearance in 1932, thanks to a man named Reginald Appleyard who developed it in the village of Ixworth, Suffolk, with the intention of producing a reliable dual-purpose fowl. Appleyard used the White Old English Game, Jubilee Indian Game, White Sussex, White Orpington, and the White Minorca to create his new breed. He succeeded in producing a fine table bird and also a good layer. The breed almost disappeared between 1950 and 1970, but now has a large following in the Shropshire area of the U.K. The plumage is always white and the birds have a pea comb, orange to red eyes, pinky-white legs and beak. A bantam was introduced in 1938, but it has now virtually disappeared. The hens tend toward broodiness. The breed prefers to be free-range.

JAVA

Despite the breed's name, the Java originated in the United States. It is one of the oldest known American chickens, and forms the basis for many other breeds. Unfortunately, this is yet another bird that is critically endangered. Javas are large birds

Black Java hen

with a sturdy appearance, making them extremely hardy. They are well suited for both meat and egg production and are highly regarded by small-scale farms and homesteads. They have a long, broad back and a deep breast. They have small earlobes and medium-sized combs and wattles, all of which are red in color. They come in three variations today—Black, Mottled and White. Javas are renowned for their foraging, which means they need less feed than many other breeds when allowed to free-range. They are docile in temperament, hardy in poor weather, and make an ideal bird for people who only want to keep a small flock.

JERSEY GIANT

The Jersey Giant is the world's largest chicken, which was developed in New Jersey, around 1870 as a dual-purpose bird. Many Jersey Giant roosters have been known to grow as large as 20 pounds. They come in three varieties—Black, White, and Blue. The Black was the first, followed by the White in the mid-twentieth century, with the Blue Laced a relatively new addition. The breed has a single bright red comb, long wattles, and earlobes with dark brown eyes. Jersey Giants are unable to fly because of their sheer size, making high boundary fences unnecessary. They do not make good pets and are slow to develop. They are, however, hardy in cold weather, calm and gentle, and the hens can lay as many as 160 large, brown eggs in one year.

NAKED NECK

The Naked Neck is one of the strangest looking chickens in the world of poultry. It looks like a cross between a turkey and a chicken, with absolutely no feathers on its neck or face. It was once referred to as a "Churkey." The exposed skin on the neck actually turns bright red when exposed to sunlight. The breed originated in Hungary, and the lack of feathers on the neck is due to a dominant gene introduced in Germany. Naked Necks are popular in countries with a hot climate because they are able to withstand higher temperatures than most chickens. They have existed as free-range birds in France for centuries, where they remain popular even today. The top of the head has feathers and most of these birds have a single comb or sometimes a rose comb and large wattles. The earlobes are red and the eyes are a reddish brown. There is also a bantam version of the Naked Neck. Apart from being an excellent table bird, Naked Necks are prolific layers and produce large, brown eggs. They are hardy birds and are happy to be free-range or confined to runs, making them ideal for smallholdings. They do, however, need protection in very cold weather because of their lack of feathers. They are easy to take care of and very placid birds. They can be found in different color varieties, including Black, White, Cuckoo, Buff, Red, and White. Because they only have around half the amount of feathers of a regular chicken, the Naked Neck is quick to pluck, which makes it another good choice for a table bird.

NEW HAMPSHIRE

This breed dates back to 1915 in the United States. New Hampshires were originally only bred for laying, but have since gained a reputation as a good table bird. The body is well rounded with a full, deep breast and a medium length tail. The breed has a single comb with five points, prominent eyes, a smooth face, large wattles and oval, red earlobes. The legs are yellow and the lower thighs are large and muscular with feet that have four toes. The feathers are a lovely deep chestnut red and are fluffy in

appearance. The hens are good layers and are both placid and friendly, making them easy to tame. They can either be left to roam free or they will adapt to being in a run, being poor fliers. They are not aggressive toward one another and do not tend toward broodiness. They can withstand cold temperatures, although you may have to watch their combs because they can be lost to frostbite.

NORFOLK GREY

The Norfolk Greay is a rare chicken that originated in the town of Norwich in Norfolk in the U.K. It is a heavy, active breed that loves to forage. The Norfolk Grey produces tinted eggs and is capable of attaining a good carcass size for meat production if allowed to mature slowly. The breed has a single comb and a red face with black eyes, while the legs are either slate or black. Plumage is attractively marked and the male has a beautiful silver hackle striped with black, as is the neck, back, saddle and wing feathers, while the rest of the plumage is a beautiful, shiny black. There is also a bantam version. Both are available in only the one color.

ORPINGTON

The Black Orpington was introduced in 1886 by William Cook who lived in Kent, England. To create it he crossed Minorcas, Plymouth Rocks, and Langshans. The White variety followed three years later, and the Buff, several years later in 1894 to satisfy the popular demand for buff-colored birds. The latter was extremely sought after and was apparently kept by the British Royal Family. Orpingtons like to be free-range and have a strong tendency to go broody. Exceptionally greedy birds, they need plenty of exercise, so holding them in a run is not really an option. They lay tinted or brown eggs, usually medium-sized. Other varieties include Jubilee, Spangled, Cuckoo, and Blue.

RHODE ISLAND RED

The Rhode Island Red (*pictured here*) is possibly the best-known breed in the world today. It is a good breed to choose if you want to keep a small number of dual-purpose chickens. Great for both egg production and for eating, Rhode Island Reds are the most prolific layers of the dual-purpose breeds. The average hen lays large brown eggs and can lay as many as 260 each year. As well as being one of the most popular breeds, the Rhode Island Red is also the most recently developed. It got its name from the state of Rhode Island in the United States, and was a combination of Brown Leghorns, Cochins, and Malays. Introduced into the U.K. in 1903, it became extremely popular very quickly. There are two different types of Rhode Island Reds, one with a double and one with a single comb. It is a very hardy bird that can withstand all kinds of conditions, and it has always proved to have a great deal of stamina. Rhode Island Reds love foraging on grass, are bright and alert, and make ideal pets. The plumage is a dark, rich, glossy red in the males, and slightly less glossy in the hens. The male should only have black in his wings and tail and the female the same, but she can have black on her neck as well. They have yellow legs and the earlobes and eyes are red.

RHODE ISLAND WHITE

The Rhode Island White originated in 1888 in the U.S.A. by crossing White Wyandottes with Partridge Cochins, and Rose Comb White Leghorns. Although a good dual-purpose bird, this never came close to the overwhelming popularity of the Rhode Island Red. It is a moderately-sized bird, with a long, broad, and deep body. The breasts are deep and well rounded, while the head is fairly deep and inclined to be flat on top. The breed generally has a rose-shaped comb, although some single combed offspring do occasionally occur. Whites are prolific layers, even in winter, and are reputed to be splendid eaters as well. They are pleasant, easy-going chickens, and make an enjoyable addition to any smallholding or as a family pet.

SCOTS DUMPY

Also known as Bakies, Crawlers, and Creepies, Dumpies have been bred in the Highlands of Scotland for over a century. They are large, low birds with a tendency to waddle as they walk due to their very short legs—no more than 2" long—hence the name "Dumpy." The tail is long and flowing and the beak is curved. Dumpies have a medium single comb that is upright and serrated. The hens make ideal mothers because they are wonderful sitters. Quiet, placid birds, they are suited to cold climates and are prolific layers even in winter. Because of their tendency to get fat, care has to be taken with their diet, but they do produce a nice amount of meat for the table. The four main varieties are Black, Cuckoo, Dark, and Silver Grey, and they come in large, bantam and miniature forms. In all varieties, the eyes are red and the comb, face, wattles, and earlobes are bright red. The beak, legs, and feet are white except for the black variety, which have slate grey or black legs. The cuckoo has mottled legs and feet.

SCOTS GREY

The Scots Grey dates back to the early sixteenth century and has been known by many different names. It is valued for its hardiness and its ability to thrive in almost any conditions. It is a long-legged, upright bird that loves to forage, and prefers to live somewhere with plenty of space. Scots Greys are good layers and produce large, whitish eggs. They can fly and prefer to roost in trees, so these birds can be quite difficult to contain. The breed comes in one color and pattern, the barred. The earlobes are red and the eyes are amber. The beak is white with black streaks, while the legs are white with black mottles.

WYANDOTTE

The Wyandotte originated in the United States but no one is certain of the breeds that were crossed to create this dual-purpose chicken. Wyandottes are famous for having a deep chest and backside that gives them a particularly rounded and pleasant appearance. It is this anatomy, however, that makes them such an excellent producer of medium brown eggs as well as juicy, moist meat. They are also renowned for their thick fleshed, bright yellow legs. The breed has a single bright red comb, bright red ear lobes and reddish eyes. The birds are suitable for either free-range or confinement in a run, but the more space they have to roam the better they will thrive. They make good pets because they are very friendly, but they can also be quite vocal, offering soft, pleasing clucks. The hens will lay around 200 eggs a year, ranging in color from brown to tinted. The birds come in many varieties–White, Blue, Buff, Red, Black, Barred, Partridge and Silver Pencilled, Silver, Gold, Blue, and Buff Laced, and finally, Columbian, which has similar markings to the Light Sussex.

BANTAMS AND SILKIES

Bantams are small fowl that are either naturally small, such as the Sebright, or birds that have been specially bred to be small. There are nearly 400 combinations of colors, shapes and features to be found in the type. Popular with people who want to start keeping a few chickens, bantams are usually ignored by commercial farms because they only lay small eggs.

The best type of bantams to keep are those that are considered "low maintenance." This means you should consider a breed that can withstand the cold, not fly over your fence, and also one that is not too aggressive toward people. In terms of being people-friendly, by far the best choice is the Astrolope. This was bred in Australia and is known for its pleasant cooing and scratching sounds. It is also very good with children and doesn't mind being picked up. Astrolopes are hardy and can stand cold weather, but the one negative aspect to this breed is that it can be quite a restless bird and prefers to be free-range. The best of the bantam layers are the Light Sussex, Rhode Island Reds, and the Anconas.

The Ancona is very friendly, but unfortunately it can fly and is not happy when kept in confined spaces. The breed does far better when it is free-range. Its main strength is that it produces a large number of white eggs even on very cold, wintry days.

If handled from a chick, the Ancona can make a perfect pet for a child. It also makes pleasant noises, so is a nice bird to have around your garden or in your yard.

One of the highest maintenance bantams is the Ardenner. The bantam version of this chicken is identical to the original larger bird. The Ardenner is not a calm presence and likes to strut and peck noisily around the run. It has long wings and can fly easily, so if you do intend to keep this breed in your garden you will need to make sure you have a very tall fence. You could spend all of your time making sure the birds don't just fly away. A peculiarity of the breed is its preference for sleeping outside all year round, in trees if possible. Ardenners also tend to hide their eggs after laying them, so if you don't fancy going on an egg hunt, this breed is probably not for you.

The Barnevelder bantam is the miniature version of the larger Dutch Barnevelder. It is a very pretty bird, being round and fluffy, but the downside is that it has a tendency to get fat and lazy. Barnevelders are possibly the worst type of bantam to keep in a coop, because they need lots of exercise, so free-range would be your best option here. If you feed them correctly, they will produce eggs right through the winter.

The Pekin bantam is a variety of true bantam chicken, which means there is no large fowl equivalent. Pekins are a little smaller than the average bantam and their feet and legs are completely covered with feathers. They are prolific foragers, so you might need to keep them away from your vegetable patch. They are round, and their plumage hangs low to the ground. Pekins are docile and easily tamed, which makes them ideal for beginners or children. They need to be kept in dry conditions because their feathered feet can accumulate mud balls that set like concrete and are extremely hard to remove. For this reason it is advisable to keep them inside during the winter or lay slabs in their run. They come in a wide variety of colors—White, Black, Blue, Splash, Buff, Buff Cuckoo, Lavender, Black Mottled, Blue Mottled, Millefleur, Silver Partridge, Gold Partridge, and Red.

Frizzles are one of the most popular and desirable bantam chickens because of their appearance. Their "backward-facing" feathers give them a striking look, almost as if they have backed up into a hair dryer. They make excellent pets because they are docile. The breed has become very popular for showing. Frizzles are also good layers, but are not broody like the Silkies. They are suitable for either free-range or outdoor pens. They have been bred in a range of colors. All colors have red eyes, a single, medium-sized comb and earlobes, but the leg color varies depending on the feather color. Beak color also corresponds with feather color. There are three types of plumage—frizzled, over-frizzled and flat-coated.

SILKIES

The Silkie, although not a true bantam, is small in size, and therefore suitable for beginners. Lightweight with a broad, stout-looking body covered in fine, fluffy feathers, Silkies have short, rather ragged-looking tails. The head is short and neat. The comb is circular and described as a mulberry comb, with short, concave, semi-circular wattles. The legs are purplish blue in color and have a fifth toe. Silkies tend to be broody and are therefore popular with breeders, especially as they make excellent foster mothers for other fowl. They are calm, friendly, and trusting little birds. They are unable to fly, so keeping them in a garden is easy. They are not great foragers and consequently do not do a lot of damage. They begin laying around Christmas time, but stop laying completely during the summer months. The eggs are light brown in color. A healthy Silkie will lay an average of 120 eggs a year. As they don't have waterproof feathers, Silkies need to be housed in dry conditions and are ideal candidates for keeping in a run. They can withstand cold and are amazingly robust, in spite of their small size. Silkies have a lifespan of around nine years and can be tamed. They make great pets for children. In fact, you only have to look at a Silkie to see why people love this breed.

AGE AND WHERE TO BUY

The age of the birds you choose to start with will depend on your situation and experience. You have a choice, so you need to consider which will suit your needs best.

HATCHING EGGS

Starting with hatching eggs is very appealing and also has many benefits if you are interested in the final egg quality. For a start you will know exactly what color your eggs will be, and with selective buying you will know more about the bird's genetics. The downside is you will need to have some equipment. If you do not already have a reliable, broody hen, then you will need to buy or borrow an incubator. It is best to buy hatching eggs directly from the breeder in person; that way you can see exactly how their birds are kept and how they select their stocks. It is not a good idea to buy hatching eggs from various sources online, unless you know the person selling them. If you do choose to go down this route, then it would be a good idea to find a breeder close enough to where you live so that you can visit them before you make your purchase. Some auctions break the law by selling hatching eggs, and buying them this way can be a considerable gamble. If you arrange for your eggs to be shipped by post, again you are running a risk because they could get damaged in transit.

DAY-OLD CHICKS

This is the cheapest way of acquiring stock, although the chicks may come unsexed which means you may have a high percentage of cockerels. This is also the most satisfying way, as you can watch them grow and get them used to handling right from the start. You will need a warm, draft-free room in which to rear them. You will also need lamps, chick crumbs, and some water. You will need to keep the temperature high, gradually reducing it as they get bigger and start to grow feathers. You will also need to keep their bedding clean at all times. There are disadvantages, of course, because if you did have a problem you risk losing the whole stock, but once you have mastered the skills you will find it a rewarding experience.

GROWERS (OR PULLETS)

This is the term used for chicks that have come away from the heat (around 8 weeks) until they are around 20 weeks. By this time the breeder will aim to have the chicks free-ranging in grass runs. Growers need to be kept apart from adult hens as they require grower's food, which has all the correct balance of nutrients to ensure they complete their growing to their fullest potential. Also there is the risk that adults can attack young birds that have not grown up with them. Growers are not difficult to look after; they just need grower food and clean, sheltered space outside with a secure house. This is a good age to buy young birds because they are usually pretty hardy if they have been well started. The added advantage of getting birds at this age is you will be able to ensure there are no cockerels among them.

POINT-OF-LAY

This is the term to describe chickens around 18 to 20 weeks old that are about to start laying. This option allows the birds to settle in to their new surroundings and you to get used to the routine. Pure breeds may be a little older (25 to 30 weeks) because they mature. Buying birds at this age means that someone else has done all the hard work of rearing them. If you already have older birds, you will need to be careful when introducing your new birds to the existing stock. Although this is the most expensive way to buy stock, you will not have to wait very long before the birds start laying.

YEAR-OLD HENS

In commercial enterprises, hens only have a productive life of one laying season. At that point, they are disposed of or sold off quite cheaply. This can be quite distressing if they have come from a battery system, becauser they will have been cooped up for a long time and they will need rehabilitating. They may be exhausted, with feathers missing and very often they have to learn how to

walk after such a long confinement. They usually undergo a complete molt when relocated at this stage of their life. This can be rewarding to someone starting out because they have the satisfaction of rescuing a bird from a life of hell and subsequent death.

WHERE TO BUY

Generally speaking, you can buy stock online, at farm stores, at farms, or from breeders.

Lovestock sales are not good places for beginners to buy poultry. If you can take with you an experienced keeper who can spot the pitfalls, this could be a viable option. When starting out it is advisable to buy from small poultry keepers who are known to be reputable breeders. You will find the larger hatcheries specialize in hybrids and may only be prepared to sell you birds in large quantities.

An auction can be a mind-boggling experience for beginners. You will be faced with cage after cage of birds marked with "dubious" breed names. The majority of the birds will be stressed. You will have no way of telling the age or health of the birds, and you are not able to examine them for lice or other diseases. You will have no proof the birds have been wormed or inoculated. Because you cannot return birds after you have bought them and they do not come with any guarantees, this is not an advisable way to buy stock if you are starting out.

Bringing Your
Chickens Home

SETTLING THEM IN

By now you will have chosen your chicken house and run, and positioned them on a suitable site. You will have food and water ready and it is now ready for occupation. All you need now are your chickens of choice and you are all set.

The ideal time to introduce your chickens to their new home is in the evening—make sure you have someone to help you just in case one of them decides to try and escape. Chickens are creatures of habit and if you just place them loose in a garden they might well decide to sleep in trees. The best way to acclimatize your chickens to their new environment is to shut them up in their house with some food and water and leave them alone for the next 24 hours. This will give them time to get used to the new smells and sights and impress on them that this is their home from now on. Once they have spent a night in the coop, they will return to it night after night. When they leave the hut for the first time, it is advisable to confine them to a run for a few days. This will give them time to orientate themselves before being allowed to wander more freely.

Whatever age the birds are when they arrive at their new home, they will probably be quite stressed from the journey. Talk to them in a calm manner and handle them as little as possible at the beginning, until they get used to you. Do everything slowly and calmly—gentle handling is essential. The correct procedure is to slip one hand under the bird and hold it firmly by both of its legs. Place two fingers between the legs, while the other hand is placed on the back to restrain the wings. When lifted up in this way, and held close to the handler's body, the bird is properly supported, minimizing any risk of damage to the wings. Only carry one bird at a time.

When introducing pullets or growers into the new house, talk to them quietly as this seems to have a calming effect. Place some on the perches and others near the drinkers, as this will help guide the other birds. Many newly housed birds need to be shown exactly where the food and water supplies are positioned. With growers, it is advisable to close off the nest boxes to stop them from sleeping in the boxes instead of on the perches provided.

Once all of the chickens are inside the house, leave them to get used to their new home. Check on them from time to time to make sure they are not panicking or having any detrimental side effects from the stress of traveling.

If it is daytime when you introduce your birds to the new house, then an hour's confinement should be enough for them to acclimatize themselves to where everything is. Then they can be released into the run with a good supply of food and water.

You will need to make sure you continue the same feeding procedure introduced by the breeder, especially if they are young birds. You can gradually introduce changes, but from an early age they should be encouraged to go outside to have a ration of grain.

LEARNING THE ROUTINE

Chickens like to stick to a regular routine, so they will expect to be let out at the same time each day. That is not to say they will all come out of the house at the same time, though: like us, some are lazier than others. Make the time you open the pop-hole a convenient time for you, one that you know you will be able to stick to without too much trouble. Once they are out in the run, check the flock for any suspicious signs such as feather pecking. If you see any bird showing signs of unusual behavior or is hunched up, then this should be dealt with straight away. The quicker you sort your problems out, the better.

Check your feeders and drinkers, and if soiled, clean them and replenish with fresh food and water. Adjust the ventilation in the house by opening windows or vents as necessary.

Make sure the birds have access to grit and crushed oyster shell; this will need to be topped up on a regular basis. Regularly check the scratching areas to make sure it is in good condition and not full of droppings. Raking it regularly not only aerates the litter, but also helps get rid of unwanted pathogens.

If your birds are free-range you will need to check the pasture regularly to see if they need to be moved to a new site. If, for example, there are a lot of bare or muddy patches, you will need to move the chickens so that the original ground can recover. If the grass is getting too long, it will need to be cut. Birds do not like long, coarse grass, particularly if it is wet, because it can make their bottom feathers wet and muddy. This, in turn, can make the eggs dirty.

Make sure you collect the eggs as soon as possible, to discourage broodiness and check for the presence of any ground-laid eggs. Remove any litter that looks as if it has been used as a nest. If any of the eggs are cracked they should be discarded immediately.

If you are around during the day it is advisable to check your birds periodically to make sure there are no problems. In the afternoon, give the birds a ration of grain, either as a scratch feed or in a grain feeder away from the house. It is a good idea to vary the place every day, so that scratching is not confined to one specific area.

As it starts to get dark the birds will return to their house, as the perching instinct is automatic. You will not usually have any problem getting your birds to roost for the night, but you may get the odd one that will stray, particularly if they are free-range and there are trees on the site. This is particularly true when the weather is warm, as some birds may want to revert to their ancestry and perch on branches. If you know your site is secure against foxes, there is usually no harm in this, but it may encourage your hens to lay eggs outside.

Once all your chickens are inside the house, close the pop-hole and leave the birds to settle down for the night.

PERIODIC ROUTINE

These are things that need to be carried out regularly, but not necessarily on a day-to-day basis. If your run has a solid floor, then you will need to make sure it is cleared of droppings. These can be put on your compost heap because they help with the breakdown of the compost. Brush out the inside of the house and replenish nest box material as necessary.

If you are moving the house to a new area, then you will need to rake the area underneath to disperse the droppings. If necessary, lime can be sprinkled on the ground while it is being rested. Birds in static houses will also need access to fresh

pasture, but that will depend on the number of birds you have and the amount of land available.

Check on feed stores regularly and buy as necessary.

THE IMPORTANCE OF LIGHTING

The amount of daylight has an important bearing on the egg laying cycle. The hormones that produce this cycle rely on the amount of light that falls on the birds' eyes. In autumn, as the amount of daylight decreases, egg production will normally start to decline, although certain breeds will continue to lay.

The importance of light has been known for a long time, and in some houses large windows are situated to provide the maximum amount of daylight. Also, traditionally the insides were painted white in order to make as much reflected light available as possible.

As long as a bird is exposed to 15 to 16 hours of light a day, she will continue to lay. In small houses, it is normally necessary to provide extra light from autumn through the winter months. The provision of light has to act in two different ways—the length of the daylight and the intensity of light. Domestic poultry keepers usually start to give artificial light to their birds when they have finished growing their feathers after the autumn molt. The intensity of light is measured with a light meter in units of "lux." Lighting can be provided in one of several ways, depending, of course, on the size of the house. On a small scale, an ordinary 25-watt bulb is enough to light a shed. If there is no electricity supply available, a portable system based on a 12-volt car battery should be sufficient to power your lighting system.

Whatever system you decide to use it is important to use a time switch so that you can control the amount of light in the house. If you want to get really technical you can use a dimming switch to warn the birds that the lights are about to go out. This is not as strange as it sounds because it gives the birds time to find their perches before it goes really dark.

There are three golden rules for lighting:

- Do not provide light before lay pullets have grown sufficiently, otherwise they will start to lay early and the eggs will be very small.

- Increase the period of light gradually until the maximum of 15 to 16 hours is reached.

- Do not allow the amount of light to get shorter once your birds have started to lay.

When providing light, start in the autumn after the molt, starting with an hour, and then gradually increasing it by half an hour a week.

THE FIRST LAY

The first signs that a hen is about to lay an egg are unmistakable. She will make a slightly moaning, almost continuous crooning sound and you will probably see her walking to and from her nesting box before she finally settles. The first egg will probably be quite small and may even be what is referred to as a "wind" egg— meaning without a yolk. This is quite common, and it may take several days for the chicken to get into its stride and lay full-sized eggs. Once the hen has laid its first egg, it will announce it to the rest of the world with the familiar cackling sound.

When the hen is going to lay, her pelvic bones will gradually move further apart. At first this distance will be about two fingers in width, widening to three our four fingers at the final stages.

As a keeper, it is important that you train the hens to lay in the nest boxes and not on the floor. You can use artificial eggs to encourage them, as well as providing a comfortable nest box liner. You need to make sure the nest boxes are in the darkest area of the house. If you do see any eggs laid on the floor, these should be removed as soon as possible.

MOLTING

Chickens molt once a year. This is the completely natural process of losing old feathers and replacing them with new ones. Chicks that hatch in the autumn or winter will molt between July and August. Those hatched after March will normally molt between October and November. Molting lasts a few weeks, and laying will decrease quite dramatically during this period.

The first indication of molting is a loss of feathers in the neck area, followed by a gradual dropping of feathers from the abdomen, back, breast and tail. Sometimes you can get a bird that may be affected by drop molting; this is where the feathers all drop out at about the same time. You will need to pay special attention to this bird, as it will be left in a weakened state leaving it prone to illness. Any bird going through a molt has to cope with extra strain on its constitution, so feeding it with extra protein, vitamins, and minerals is particularly important at this stage.

CHICKENS AND CHILDREN

Children are always fascinated by animals, and chickens are no exception. What makes it even more interesting is that the chickens are often just as curious about children as the children are about them. If you have young children and they frequently play in the garden you might want to allow them each their own allotted space. A chicken can easily get spooked by a bunch of noisy children kicking a soccer ball around, which might cause them to become nervous or even aggressive. So right from the start it is a good idea to educate your children on how to behave around the chickens. Once

they learn to be calm and quiet in the presence of the birds, you can then show them the best way to pick up the chickens. Get them to practice until they are comfortable, and stress the importance of not dropping the birds. Although hens are hardy, they are also fragile, so until your children are confident handling the chickens, make sure they are always supervised.

You can gradually introduce other aspects of taking care of them and allow children to hand-feed your hens treats of lettuce.

Because E. coli can be carried in the chickens' droppings, make sure children wear gloves when they are handling the birds or cleaning out a run or coop. Alternatively, make sure they wash their hands properly afterward. Thankfully, E. coli is not robust enough to cope with a good dose of soap and hot water.

Children enjoy spending time with chickens and it is a way of getting kids outside in the fresh air, away from the television or computer screen. Chickens make great pets and are intelligent as well as educational. Children can learn all about egg production and can help you collect the eggs each morning. Imagine the delight on their faces when they see the chickens marching back into the coop at the end of the day in single file or handling the first chicks as they arrive.

COPING WITH THE WORST JOBS

CLIPPING WINGS

This isn't as painful or cruel as it sounds. Chickens do not fly as well as other birds, but they can flap their wings enough to carry them over fences and out of the coop. If you are intending to leave your chickens free-range, then clipping their wings is a must. You do not want them to escape because they could easily get in trouble with an angry dog, a fox, or some other predator in the area. It is also not a good idea if they keep escaping into your neighbor's garden.

Clipping wings can be a bit daunting if you have never done it before. However, once you have got the hang of it you will soon find out it is not nearly as difficult or dangerous as you originally imagined. Have a pair of sharp scissors to hand and follow these basic instructions. You will only need to clip one wing. If you clip both, a lighter bird will simply flap harder and still manage to get into the air. By only clipping one, they become unbalanced and are unable to fly.

1. *Catch the chicken.* This is probably the hardest part about clipping chicken wings. Some chickens are quite docile and do not mind being handled at all, while others fear humans and run as if their lives depend on it. The easiest thing is to try and get it in a corner, so it has nowhere to run. You can also use a towel and throw it over the chicken, which should slow it down enough to enable you to grab it. Once you have hold of the chicken, apply gentle pressure to the wings and then pick it up. It is always a good idea to handle your chickens as much as possible so they get used to the idea, then you won't have to be so worried about being pecked or clawed.

2. *Invert and calm the chicken.* Now you need to spend a minute or two calming the chicken down. Pet it gently, talk softly to it, and then turn it upside down. For some reason this seems to put them into a trance and they immediately become much more docile.

3. *Expose the wing.* With the chicken still upside down, choose which wing you are going to clip. Expose the primary feathers by taking hold of the wing and gently pulling it away from the chicken's body. You will be able to tell the primary flight feathers from the others because they will be a different colour and they are generally longer. They are the 10 or so feathers closest to the tip of the chicken's wing.

4. *Cut back the primary feathers.* Using a pair of clean, sharp scissors. Clip around two thirds of the length of the first 10 or so feathers on the chicken's wing. Take a look

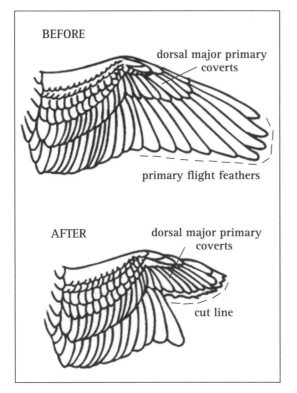

BEFORE

dorsal major primary coverts

primary flight feathers

AFTER

dorsal major primary coverts

cut line

at the diagram above to see roughly how much of the feather you should be cutting off. It also shows the dorsal major primary coverts to act as a guide. The idea is to take enough of the feather off without making it bleed.

Chicken feathers have veins extending into them about 1" or so. If you cut below this point, the feather is completely dead and the chicken feels nothing, much like cutting our own nails. However, if you cut above this point the chicken will begin to bleed through the cut feather, which will leave the chicken open to infection. If this does happen, apply a little pressure to the

tip of the feather with a clean cloth, and take your chicken to a vet. If you cut the primary feathers carefully, there is no reason why you should ever cause your chickens any pain or distress.

5. *Release the chicken.* Once you have successfully trimmed the chicken's feathers, release it. You might find it is a little disoriented for a moment, but it will quickly recover.

HUMANE CULLING

If you decide to keep chickens for meat as well as eggs, there will come the time when you have to do the job that most beginners hate—culling. It goes without saying that you will want to do it in the most humane way possible. To carry out the job properly you need to be sure you are mentally able to go through with it, and that you apply the task in an appropriate and quick way. If you follow these simple instructions, hopefully the task won't seem too daunting.

1. Your main aim in culling a chicken is to remain totally calm at all times, so as not to distress any of the birds. Go into the coop after dark, carrying a red lamp, talking softly or even whistling so the birds know it is you. This means they won't panic and upset everything. Slowly approach the bird you want to cull and simply take it by the legs from the perch and pull it into your side by placing a hand around its body and then cup its head in your hand. Then walk quietly away from the coop with the bird tucked under your arm.

2. Take your right hand and slide it under the bird's bottom and grasp its legs. With the hand closed, take the legs with the thumb pointing away from the body, because this is a much stronger grip.

3. Next cup the head in the palm of your hands with the middle fingers pointing away from the beak and the top of the head in the palm of the hand. Carefully and forcefully pull downward on the head and then twist in one clean movement. You will feel the head part from the body as the neck is broken.

4. As you release the pressure the bird will start to flap uncontrollably, but there is no need to panic as the bird cannot feel any pain because the messages are not getting through to the brain. This is merely a spasm that will stop in about 30 seconds.

5. You can hang the bird for a day or two if you wish, or you can go straight to the next stage—plucking. Hanging means that the blood will pool in the neck end so that draining is unnecessary.

PLUCKING
Get a bucket of really hot water—too hot for you to put your hands in—then dip in the bird and count to 60. Take it out and start by plucking the wing feathers, followed by the legs and breast. The feathers will all come out easily as the hot water melts the fat that is around the pen of the feather, making it almost fall out.

EVISCERATION
Eviscerating a chicken is the process of removing the insides, or gutting, but it is one of those things that is much easier to show someone than to write it down. Hopefully, this will give you some idea of how to prepare your chicken for the oven.

1. After the chicken has been plucked, remove the feet, using a knife.

2. Slip a knife under the skin at the bottom of the neck and cut up to the head. Sever the neckbone at the bottom end with a pair of secateurs or a sharp knife. Save it for soup or stock.

3. Remove the neckbone. Insert the index finger of your right hand, move it around inside, and sever all of the innards.

4. Cut between the vent and the tail, being careful not to sever the rectum. Cut right round the vent so as to separate it from the body. Carefully draw the vent, with the guts attached, out of the tail end. The gizzard, lungs, and heart will all follow. Finally, remove the crop from the neck end of the bird.

BEHAVIORAL PROBLEMS

Even the best-kept birds can run afoul of behavioral problems and this section explains the causes and cures for the most common ones that you will come across.

THE PECKING ORDER

Chickens, like many other creatures, live by a well-defined order of hierarchy known as the "pecking order." Each bird has its own place on the social ladder and can dominate those of lower standing. There is a "top bird" to which the rest will show great respect, often giving way at the food container or generally getting out of their way. This top bird is generally a cockerel, but in the absence of a male, an old hen will probably hold the position. You will notice the dominant bird will often raise its hackles—much the same way as a dog who feels threatened—this is a way of showing disapproval and that it will attack if a subordinate does not show respect. If you are close enough you may be able to hear a low growling noise, warning the other chicken to keep its distance. The pecking order extends downward, just as it does in human societies, with the weakest having to survive as best they can. You may find that a weakened bird that is either injured or sick can fall prey to attacks, particularly if the other chickens believe it is not worthy of being in the flock.

You may not notice there is a visible pecking order within your birds, but it will become evident if you try to introduce new birds to an existing flock. There are always problems because the natural pecking order has been disrupted. A hen spotting a newcomer will utter a single warning croak that alerts the flock. It then becomes a challenge to the existing birds to peck at and chase away the stranger.

Coping with the pecking order

Although you will never be able to alter the pecking order, you can help the trouble it causes by taking a few preventative measures. Firstly, it is essential you give your birds enough room to roam without any overcrowding, not only to allow them to forage but also to stop boredom from setting in. Keeping compatible breeds of the same age together in a pen can help stop bullying by older, more dominant birds. A good diet of nutritious food and making sure your birds are healthy can also reduce the negative impact of the hierarchy. If you are aware you have a particularly bossy hen, you can sometimes influence her status by removing her from the others and placing her in a separate pen for a week. When she is reintroduced to the flock, she will be at the bottom of the pecking order and will consequently need to re-establish herself—usually lower down the social ladder.

If it is absolutely essential to introduce new birds to an existing flock, they should be placed in temporary pens next to the existing run so that they can be seen by the other hens, but cannot be attacked. It will also be necessary to have a separate shelter for them during this period—about 1 to 2 weeks—and you should place the food for each set of birds on either side of the boundary. This means they will be feeding in close proximity, but they will not be able to attack and give them time to get used to one another. Once the birds seem to take each other for granted, you can amalgamate the flocks. Keep a careful eye for any potential problems during the first couple of days. If you do see any problems, you can initiate a program of disorientation. This is where the original flock is put in the temporary pen, while the new birds are given the original quarters. This is usually very effective as they all take time to adjust to their new surroundings and forget about challenging the other birds.

FEATHER-PECKING

It is not uncommon for a chicken to damage its own plumage by pecking at its own feathers. This can lead to a serious problem of abnormal aggression, because once blood starts to flow the other birds will become excited and it can lead to cannibalism. Feather-pecking is not confined to domestic hens; it is also common among pheasants, turkeys, partridges, parrots, and a variety of other birds. The severity of feather-pecking in poultry flocks can range from the bird just pecking out the odd feather while preening, to an aggressive form where birds will peck each other to the extreme.

Causes of feather-pecking
- Mixing incompatible breeds together.
- Introducing an ex-battery hen, who will bring a bad habit with it.
- Injured or molting birds.
- Illness in the flock or an underdeveloped runt.
- An infestation of lice or mites can cause a hen to peck its own feathers to relieve the itching.
- Lack of nutrients, poor diet or water, might lead the bird to search for nutrients from its own feathers.
- Keeping more than one cockerel in close proximity can lead to bullying and fighting.

- Overcrowding or boredom.
- Introducing new stock or aggressive birds to an existing pecking order.
- The incorrect use of artificial light in the hen house, which can lead to stress.

Cures

- Apply a nasty-tasting substance such as mustard or Stockholm tar to the affected area.
- Buy a proprietary, natural cereal-based product called Pecka-Block, or a similar product, to help reduce feather pecking.
- Most commercial farms practice beak-trimming, which is the removal of the pointed tip of the upper beak. This does prevent feather-pecking but you will need to bear in mind that this can also stop your hens from eating certain foods such as the tips of grass blades and other small morsels of food.
- Make sure your birds have plenty of space and there is adequate foraging material available.
- If you are using artificial lighting, reduce the light intensity inside the coop.
- If one bird is particularly bad—especially if there is blood present—it is advisable to place it in a hospital pen until it has fully recovered. Make sure it has access to plenty of food and water.
- Help your chickens to recover from molting quickly by feeding them extra protein (for example, meal worms) and other supplements.

EGG EATING

Once your chickens have started eating their own eggs and those of others, it is a habit that is very hard to break, and will very often spread to the rest of the flock. It is much easier to stop it before it starts. This habit often starts by accident after an egg with a particularly soft shell breaks, or an egg gets crushed. Unfortunately, once a hen gets a taste for eggs, it will deliberately crack the shells and have a nightly feast.

Causes of egg eating

- Overcrowding is one of the main factors, because the birds get bored and start fighting.
- Illness and poor diet usually means the birds are not getting enough calcium, which affects the quality of the shells.
- If a bird is at the bottom of the pecking order and isn't allowed access to food, it will seek nourishment in other ways.
- If the area surrounding the nest box is too light, the hen might become inquisitive. A hen's natural instinct is to lay in the dark in a secret place.
- If there are not enough nest boxes or nesting material available for the number of hens in the house, this could lead to fighting and some of the eggs getting broken.
- If chickens are fed their own shells as a calcium supplement, you might find they acquire the taste and develop the habit.

Cures

- Feed the hens extra calcium in the form of oyster shell to make sure that the eggs have strong shells.
- Make sure nest boxes are in the darkest area of the coop.
- Change the nest box design, so the eggs slide out of sight and reach. Slope the base so the egg rolls to the back of the nest box into a container filled with some soft material such as straw.
- If you notice a problem at feeding time, make sure you have enough feeders to allow the ones at the bottom of the pecking order to get their fair share.
- If you find you cannot stop a certain bird from eating her eggs, then the only answer is to permanently isolate the egg eater so it does not influence the rest of the flock.
- Make sure the eggs are regularly collected throughout the day, removing any temptation.

BROODINESS

All animals have the natural instinct to become broody, and chickens are no exception. In fact one of the strongest instinctive behaviors chickens display is broodiness. A broody hen has an overwhelmingly motherly desire to sit on and incubate her eggs after they are laid. This is very common and something most chicken keepers will have to deal with. Some breeds are more prone to it than others so it is quite a good idea to start with breeds such as the Welsummer, Leghorn, or Ancona, who don't usually go broody at all. Hens can become broody around two to three times a year, and this is usually in the spring and summer, so if you want the optimum amount of eggs you will need to recognize the signs.

It isn't always easy to predict exactly which hen, if any, is going to become broody. Start to watch for signs in the spring and particularly in birds that are in their second year of life. It is also more likely to happen if the eggs are not collected on a regular basis.

How to spot a broody hen

A broody hen will happily sit and stay in the nest box for the majority of the day and night. Every time you try to go near her she may fluff up her feathers and make an unusual noise. You will probably find she becomes quite anxious and bad-tempered, and will probably attempt to peck anyone who goes near her nest as she tries to protect her clutch. A broody hen will usually make a quick dash to the feeders and drinkers and possibly take a rapid dustbath before returning to the nest. Hens will often pull out the feathers from their undercarriage to allow the heat from their body to reach the eggs more efficiently. So keep an eye out for any loose feathers in the bottom of the nest. Unfortunately, the broody chicken doesn't know she is wasting her time, as a hen who hasn't had an encounter with a cockerel will not be caring for a fertilized egg.

Harmful effects of broodiness
Sitting on her eggs day after day is not only bad for the hen in question, but also for any other chickens within the flock. She will probably lose condition as she neglects to look after herself, and some chickens are reluctant to move at all when they become broody. As they remain static they become prone to parasitic infestations, particularly in the warmer months. If you only have a limited space with a few nest boxes, this can upset the other hens if one of the nests is constantly occupied. This in itself can lead to bullying. The nest box usually becomes very dirty and you will notice a general disruption to the normal status quo in the chicken house.

How to discourage broodiness
The best way to stop your hens from becoming broody is regular removal of the eggs. Make sure you do it at least once a day, but the more often the better. If you notice one of your hens is going broody, try to encourage her out of the hen house by physically picking her up and placing her outside the pop-hole. If you find she constantly returns to the nest then you might need to take more drastic measures, such as actually blocking off the nesting box or placing objects inside that will

discourage her from sitting. However, some hens have a strong instinct toward broodiness and you may need to remove them to a temporary accommodation in a cooler place for a few days. The change of environment and conditions should soon take her mind off sitting on eggs all day. Whatever happens, don't delay in taking some form of action—the longer you leave it, the harder the habit is to break.

Encouraging broodiness
Of course, if you would like to replace old stock or add to your existing flock by having chicks, then broodiness is not a negative thing. It is far more natural to allow a broody hen to raise your chicks than placing them in an artificial incubator. If you want to encourage a hen to become broody it is a good idea to place some artificial eggs in a nest box to encourage her to sit. Make sure the nest area is safe and secure from the other chickens, as it is not uncommon for a more dominant hen within the group to exert her authority. See the section on Raising Your Own Chicks on page 93, for more details.

Feeding

FEEDING REQUIREMENTS

As long as you provide your chickens with plenty of food and clean water, and the ability to forage on pasture from time to time, there is no reason why they should not live happy and potentially full lives.

As we have seen on page 20 when discussing the internal organs of a chicken, they have no teeth. The beak can break food into easily swallowed pieces, but that is all it can do—there is no chewing motion involved at all. The food you give your chicken needs to provide everything the bird requires to maintain the correct working of its metabolism and, in particular, its immune system.

Nutritional requirements are essentially the same throughout the chicken's life, and only the quantity and proportion will differ as it develops. For example, growing chicks will need more protein in their first few weeks of life than an adult bird. The table opposite shows the nutrients required, their function, and the main sources thereof.

You can usually tell if you are feeding a balanced diet to your chickens by the state of their droppings. The ideal dropping should be slightly fluffy in appearance, semi-solid, not runny, and white in parts. If you do find that the droppings are yellow and runny then it could be for the following reasons.

- Too much protein
- Presence of parasites
- Sudden change of diet or environment
- Illness

AMOUNT OF FEED

As a guide, a laying hen will require 3 1/2 to 5 ounces of balanced layer's mash per day. This will of course depend on her size and the number of eggs she lays. Layer's mash is a completely balanced diet, so the only other thing she will need is water.

If you are not feeding your chickens exclusively on a proprietary mash, then you will also need to provide some grain. An average daily intake would be 2 1/2 to 3 ounces of balancer pellets and 1 to 2 ounces of whole grain. Balancer pellets are intended to be fed with the grain because they have the perfect balance of ingredients to supplement the grain. Remember, grain must be clean and dry—anything damp and showing signs of mold should be discarded because it can kill the birds.

You can also feed your chickens scraps from your kitchen with the balancer pellets,

Nutrient	Function	Main sources
Proteins	Body building and repair	Fish meal, blood meal, soya, skim milk
Carbohydrates	Energy	All cereal grains
Fats and oils	Energy	Fish meal, meat and bone meal, groundnuts (peanuts)
Vitamin A	Normal growth, disease resistance	Grass meal, yellow maize meal
Vitamin B complex	Optimum growth rate and production	Fish meal, yeast, skim milk, cereals
Vitamin D	Healthy growth, prevention of rickets, strong eggshells	Sunlight, fish meal, cod liver oil
Vitamin K	Healthy blood	Grass meal
Calcium and Phosphorous	Healthy bones and strong eggshells	Meat, fish meal, bonemeal, limestone flour
Zinc	Healthy skin and feather development	Available in supplements
Manganese	Strong eggshells, good hatching rate	Available in supplements
Iodine	Control of metabolism	Seaweed extract, available as a supplement

and this should be around 1 1/2 ounces per bird. If you are feeding layer's mash cut the quantity down to about 1 ounce. If you feed your chickens entirely on kitchen scraps and grain, the level of egg production will fall drastically, so only use them as a supplement to the other food. If you allow your hens to run out of doors, or have access to a wide variety of foods, they will balance their own rations and not eat more than they need.

WHAT TO FEED

Because the hen has to use so much energy to produce an egg—which is like a pure lump of protein in itself—that protein needs to be replaced through its diet. When feeding chickens it is important to make sure you feed the correct proportion of grains and proteins and most proprietary mixes have the balance right. Earthworms are a very good source of protein for chickens, so allowing them to forage in the garden will be a good supplement to their daily diet. Alternatively, you could start your own wormery and feed them worms in their run, if you are not intending to allow them to roam free-range.

Ready-mixed feeds provide all the essential nutrients in their correct balance, and can be bought to suit fowl at all stages of their lives. They come in powder, crumbs or pellets and can be fed wet or dry.

Two things that concern the smallholder about buying proprietary feed is the cost—they can be expensive—and the fact that many of these mixes contain antibiotics. While these may be necessary to counteract infection where intensive farming is involved, for the average poultry keeper who likes to rear his or her chickens in a more natural state, these antibiotics are not so important.

GREEN FEED

Hens love to eat vegetables and other greenstuff. It not only acts as a source of

Potatoes	Boiled and added to mash—do not use green ones
Jerusalem artichokes	Cooked or minced raw
Grass mowings	Given dried or green
Brassicas	Given green
Turnips	Tops fed green; roots cooked or minced raw
Carrots	Cooked or minced raw
Groundsel	Fed green
Acorns	Dried and crushed
Nettle tops	Only pick young tops. Boil with potatoes or scraps
Parsley	Fed green
Beans (all types)	Dried and ground up
Lettuce	Only use ones that have gone to seed and feed whole
Fruit	Small quantities given fresh but avoid citrus fruits
Broccoli	Boiled and added to mash
Cucumber	Feed raw
Tomatoes	Feed ripe tomatoes raw

supplementary nutrients but it also helps to relieve the boredom. Greens and vegetables are not high in energy and should not be substituted for large amounts of the diet. Some vegetables need to be boiled before being given as food—the chart on the left will give you a guide as to how they can be used. Large vegetables, such as cabbages, can be suspended in the run so the chickens can reach up and peck at them. Other green feeds can be chopped up and added to the mash or given whole for the hens to peck at will. Weeds and grass mowings are also acceptable, provided you haven't used any pesticides or weedkillers on them. If your hens do not eat all the greenstuff in one go, make sure you clear it out of the run as it can quickly decay and be bad for their digestion.

Onion tops, chives and finely chopped garlic are useful as disease and worm preventatives, although it is advisable to use them sparingly as they can impart flavors to the eggs.

SPROUTED GRAINS

Another good source of winter food for egg layers is sprouted grain. Any grains can be used, but the ones that are easiest to obtain are wheats or oats. Allow 1 pound of grain for every 30 hens and leave it to soak in lukewarm water for at least 24 hours. Drain off the water and continue to sprinkle with water every morning and evening until the grains start to sprout. Spread them out on a clean surface and continue sprinkling until the sprouts are about 1" long. Stop sprinkling with water and allow them to dry off, but don't allow them to go moldy because you will have to throw them away if that happens. They can either be fed with grain as a scratch feed or chopped up and added to the mash.

FEEDING CALCIUM AND GRIT

For shells to form properly they need plenty of calcium, and if you don't intend to use proprietary feeds with supplements added, you will need to add these yourself. Crushed oyster shell is available to buy, as is limestone grit, and if you put a container of each of these in the chickens' run, they can help themselves when they need it. Another source of calcium is recycled egg shells. The drawback to this is that if you leave any pieces of shell that are recognizable to the hen, it can encourage an egg eating habit. You can get round this by baking the shells to sterilize them before grinding them up very finely.

As explained earlier, grit is needed to aid with the chickens' digestion in the gizzard. This can be fed in the form of small pieces of flint or gravel. If your hens are free-range they should be able to find adequate quantities of grit, but if they are confined to a run you will need to provide it for them at the rate of half an ounce per bird. Oyster shell also acts as a good source of grit, as well as providing calcium and phosphorous.

WATER

Chickens, like all living creatures, need fresh, clean water to survive. This is not surprising when you consider that 70 percent of the hen's weight is water, and 65 percent in their eggs. Five chickens will drink approximately 1 quart of water a day in normal conditions, but they will drink twice this amount when the weather is hot. If you do not supply enough water, not only will their eggs be smaller, but you could trigger an outbreak of egg eating.

The temperature of the water is important as well. If the water is too warm the hens tend to ignore it as it does not help to cool their body temperature to the required 104°F. It is only when the water is cool that the hens seem to drink on a regular basis. So make sure you change their water regularly when the weather is hot and the waterer is shaded to avoid the water getting too warm. Large units will usually require an automatic water supply, but manual waterers are ideal for the smaller units. In the winter make sure that the water doesn't become frozen, so again you will need to top up your waterers on a regular basis.

MIXING YOUR OWN FEED

You may decide you want to go the whole hog and mix your own feed, in which case follow the guidelines on the opposite page. If you are raising chickens then chick crumbs are a complete food that will provide everything a growing chick needs from day-old to six or eight weeks. Because the balance has been specially worked out in this type of feed, it is advisable to use this on your young chicks to give them a good start in life. After six to eight weeks you can turn to a more natural method if you prefer.

Once a chick reaches around six to eight weeks, it requires less protein in its diet so it can adapt more easily to an organic diet. Whichever way you choose to feed your chickens make sure any changes you make to their diet are gradual otherwise you risk upsetting your flock and causing health problems.

A good way of supplementing your chickens' diet is to make your own mash from leftover kitchen scraps. Sunday is a good day to make the mash as you can use the leftover water used to boil the vegetables as the base for your mashstock. Add everything you have saved from the week to the pot, bring to the boil and

GENERAL FORMULA FOR HOME MIXES

| | pounds/100 pounds of mix | | |
	Starter	Grower	Layer
Coarsely ground grain (corn, milo, barley, oats, wheat, rice, etc.)	43	50	53
Wheat bran, mill feed, rice bran, milling by-products etc.	9	17.5	16.5
Soybean meal	36	16.5	15.5
Meat meal, fish meal (soybean meal may be substituted for either of these)	5	5	3
Alfalfa meal (can be left out if fresh pasture is available)	4	4	4
Yeast, milk powder (can be left out if vitamin supplement is properly balanced)	2	2	2

(Vitamin supplement must provide 200,000 I.U. of Vitamin A, 80,000 I.C.U. of Vitamin D, and 100 mg of riboflavin)

	Starter	Grower	Layer
Salt with trace minerals. (Trace mineral salt or iodized salt supplemented with 1/2 ounce each of manganese sulfate and zinc oxide)	8 ounces	8 ounces	8 ounces
Bone meal, deflourinated dicalcium phosphate	>.05	>.05	>.05
Ground limestone, oyster shells	>.01	>.01	>.05

gently simmer for a while until it becomes a stodgy mash. Here is a rough guide of items that are suitable for putting into your mash:

Artichoke
Beans—runner, broad, dwarf, haricot, etc.
Beetroot
Broccoli
Cabbage
Carrots
Corn
Kale
Leeks
Lettuce
Corn
Onions
Peas
Potatoes
Spinach
Sunflower seeds
Swedes
Turnips

Other leftovers of the non-vegetable type can include:

Biscuits
Bread
Cake
Cooked pasta
Cooked rice
Leftover meat
Old breakfast cereals

FEED MANAGEMENT

To maintain healthy birds, their food needs to be fresh at all times. It is advisable to limit the amount of feed in feeders to avoid waste, so this might need a bit of trial and error. Fill non-automatic trough feeders in the early morning and during the day whenever feed supplies get low. If there is any leftover feed in the trough it should be removed before refilling.

It is good management to keep a record of your birds' weight and their feed consumption. A drop-in feed intake is usually one of the first signs of trouble—an outbreak of disease, molting, stress, or poor management.

If you are buying preparatory food, then keep it as fresh as possible. It is probably advisable not to order too large a quantity at any one time, if possible reorder every couple of weeks. Make sure the feed store is dry and rat- and mouse-proof. A large metal trash can with a tight lid makes an excellent storage container.

Although feed is the biggest expense of keeping poultry, it is unfortunately, vital to keep your hens laying at a good rate. As explained earlier buying the commercial brands of food will provide your chickens with all the nutrients and proteins they need, but new keepers should still be encouraged to blend at least some proportion of their own feed.

A–Z of Pests and Diseases

GENERAL WELL-BEING

Most problems associated with poultry can be avoided by simply paying adequate attention to hygiene, feeding, and the general care of your birds. However, even under the most carefully controlled conditions, disease can still occur.

A healthy bird is normally alert, curious, interested in its food and surroundings, bright-eyed, and walking with an upright stance. If you see one of your birds standing in a dejected, drooping position or huddled up inside its feathers, then you need to isolate the bird as quickly as possible. It is handy to keep a small pen purely for this purpose, where you can isolate the sick bird and keep an eye on it for a few days. Symptoms to look out for are diarrhea, lack of appetite, coughing, wheezing, runny nose, discharge from the eyes, lameness, trembling, sudden pecking of the feathers, or any other unusual behavior. Make sure you wash your hands thoroughly after handling any sick birds, to avoid spreading the problem to the rest of the flock.

This section gives you a list of diseases and problems you may come across as a poultry keeper and possible treatments. Before you embark on poultry-keeping, make sure you know of a vet in your area that has a good knowledge on the subject. Avian vets can be hard to find, but if you ask advice from a professional poultry keeper, they should be able to give you some guidance.

DISEASES
Aspergillosis
Aspergillosis is also known as Brooder Pneumonia or Farmer's Lung and is caused by the birds inhaling fungus spores (*Aspergillus fumigatus*) either from moldy litter, nesting, or food. The symptoms are excessive thirst, rapid breathing, gasping, inflamed eyes, and an overall depressed posture. Young birds are particularly at risk and there is no known cure, although antibiotics have in some cases shown to produce an improvement. To avoid this condition you will need to adhere to a strict hygiene routine, avoiding any damp hay, straw, wood shavings, and feed, together with good management of litter. This condition can also affect human beings.

Avian encephalomyelitis
Avian encephalomyelitis is caused by a virus transmitted primarily through the egg. The

only effective control is by vaccination of breeders. The disease is mainly seen in chicks between 1 and 3 weeks old and you will notice their movements are restricted and their heads and necks will visibly tremble. Breeding flocks that are affected will acquire an immunity, but no eggs should be incubated from them for several weeks until this is established.

Avian influenza

Avian influenza is caused by airborne viruses and affects the bird's respiratory tract, much the same way as a cold does in a human. You might notice a slight swelling of the head and neck, and more often than not there is a nasal discharge. There are two main forms of this disease, distinguished by low and high extremes of virulence. The so-called low pathogenic form commonly causes only mild symptoms (ruffled feathers, a drop in egg production) and may easily go undetected. The highly pathogenic form is far more dramatic. It spreads rapidly through poultry flocks, causes disease affecting multiple internal organs and has a mortality rate that can approach 100 percent within 48 hours. There is no treatment for avian influenza, but mortality rate is low in the mild form of this disease.

Avian tuberculosis

Avian tuberculosis is a chronic wasting disease caused by infection with *Mycobacterium avum*. All species of birds are susceptible, with domestic fowl the most frequently infected. Birds of all ages may be affected, but it is older birds that are the most vulnerable to this disease. Symptoms are gradual wasting especially evident as atrophy of the pectoral muscles, tiredness, dull and ruffled plumage, jaundice, lameness, or dropping of wing and diarrhea. You will need to seek the advice of a bird vet because there is no cure for this disease, and he may suggest it is best to cull the entire flock.

Blackhead

This disease, more correctly called *histomoniasis*, is primarily a disease of young turkeys. Chickens seem to be more resistant to the effects of the infection but may act as carriers. Blackhead is caused by a microscopic protozoan called *Histomonas meleagridis*, which is transmitted via water, feed, or droppings. Infected eggs of the parasitic caecal worm, *Heterakis gallinarum*, are also a source of infection.

The first signs of this disease are a decrease in feed consumption and consequent loss of weight. Sick birds appear dull and depressed, and often stand by themselves with dropping tails, ruffled feathers, and a sleepy appearance. You may also notice their droppings are a sulfur yellow color. If birds are not treated, or if treatment is delayed, mortality can be very high. The drug Dimetridazole can be used in the drinking water or feed to control outbreaks of histomoniasis. It is important that you do not allow the ground to become over-used, or to have chickens and turkeys sharing the same land. The periodic moving of feeders, waterers and roosts should help prevent the local buildup of infectious organisms. Good sanitation and litter management will also help prevent transmission of the caecal worm and the blackhead organism.

Botulism

Botulism is a condition where birds lose control of their neck muscles and is commonly referred to as Limber Neck. It is caused by a bacteria (*Clostridium botulinum*), which is found in decaying organic matter. It is more common in waterfowl than in poultry, because of their tendency to dabble in mud, although losses of domestic waterfowl are much lower than those sustained in the wild. If you diagnose it in time, a teaspoon of Epsom salts dissolved in 1 1/2 teaspoons of water may improve the condition and eventually bring about a full recovery. It is important to remove any decaying vegetation from pools and runs, and to maintain high standards of cleanliness. Clinical signs in poultry and wild birds are similar—flaccid paralysis of the legs, wings, neck, and eyelids. Chickens that have succumbed to botulism show signs of ruffled feathers and diarrhea.

Bumblefoot

Bumblefoot is the common name for a swelling that results from an infected cut or graze on the underside of the foot. The wound heals on the outside, but leaves a hard core of pus on the inside. It is sometimes found where birds are provided with perches that are too high for them, or where they are grazing on flinty ground. The affected bird will have a limp and, on examination of the foot, you will see evidence of a hard abscess. Applying slight pressure is sometimes enough to burst it, releasing the pus, but it may require lancing with a sterilized blade. Antiseptic or hydrogen peroxide should then be applied to the affected area. Keep the bird isolated in a clean straw pen for a few days until the wound has healed. All birds can be affected by bumblefoot, but it is most common among chicken and ducks.

Caecal worms

Caecal worms, *Heterakis gallinae*, are nematode parasites of poultry and game birds. They are small, whitish worms with a pointed tail, up to 1/2" in length, that live in the caecum. They do not cause disease, although their eggs are capable of transmitting Blackhead. They can be easily controlled by means of a poultry wormer such as Flubendazole or Levamisole.

Chronic Respiratory Disease

Just like humans, poultry are susceptible to the common cold and can show signs of sneezing, coughing, and wheezing. It is initially caused by a viral infection, followed by a secondary bacterial invasion of the organism *Mycoplasma gallisepticum*. Make sure your chicken houses are well-ventilated without being drafty and try to maintain a stress-free management system. Mild cases, where secondary infection is only slight, will clear up fairly quickly, but severe cases may require treatment by antibiotics. The symptoms can appear similar to those of Newcastle disease and infectious bronchitis, so if you are in any doubt consult your avian vet.

Cloacitis

Cloactis is commonly found in hens allowed to run indiscriminately with infected males. Ideally the sexes should be kept apart unless controlled breeding is required. The signs of this contagious venereal disease are swollen membranes in the cloaca, with a whitish discharge. The affected bird should be separated from the rest of the flock, and its vent area painted with iodine.

Coccidiosis

Coccidiosis is one of the most important poultry diseases, caused by protozoal parasites (*coccidia*) that live in the lining of the intestine. The condition most commonly occurs under intensive rearing conditions, but it is possible for this disease to affect most poultry systems, both indoor and outdoor. The disease is usually seen in birds of 3 to 6 weeks old, before they have received immunity. Infected birds will have ruffled feathers and a breakdown in intestinal function, their head drawn back into their shoulders and a chilled appearance. The first recognizable symptom of cocidiosis is blood in the droppings, with the most virulent strains causing diarrhea and subsequent death. Poultry are exposed to the parasite via their droppings, dirty drinkers, and damp litter in their houses. Separate affected poultry and use medicated feed and water.

Coryza

Coryza is an acute, sometimes chronic, highly infectious disease of chickens that occasionally affects pheasants and guinea-fowl. It is characterized by a catarrhal inflammation of the upper respiratory tract, nasal discharge, facial swelling, loss of appetite, and a drop in egg production. It is caused by the bacterium *Haemophilus paragallinarum*. Severe cases may require antibiotic treatment but the mortality rate is generally low.

Cramp

There is not much known about cramp, which seems to affect ducks more than any other poultry. The cause could possibly be fatigue, lack of exercise, faulty feeding or cold conditions. The first indication is when a duck is found to be hobbling badly and swinging its tail over to one side in an effort to keep its balance. If the condition is severe, the duck may not be able to walk at all. The best course of action is to isolate the duck in a sheltered place in a straw-lined pen until it recovers. It is thought this condition can also be brought on by a deficiency in calcium or Vitamin D, in which case supplements of these can be included in the treatment.

Dropped wing

Dropped wing is most frequently found in geese, although it has been known to occur in ducks as well. It is a result of muscular weakness that makes the wing hang down lower than normal in its resting position. Although the condition is unsightly it does not appear to cause any distress and is completely harmless to the bird.

Duck virus hepatitis

Duck virus hepatitis is a highly infectious disease and fatal condition affecting young ducklings. The first indication of this disease is when the bird's movements seem to be wobbly and uneven. There is no cure, but there is a preventive vaccine. Rats have been reported as a reservoir host of the virus so pest control is strongly advised.

Egg binding

Egg binding is when a bird produces an egg but is unable to lay it. There can be several reasons for this and it should be treated seriously. Seek the help of an avian vet as soon as you suspect that your bird might be egg bound. The symptoms include sitting on the floor for long periods of time and excessive straining. There will also be a swollen area around her vent and her droppings will be much larger. The bigger the dropping gets, the closer the egg is to the cloacae, where it is due to be expelled. Egg binding is a serious condition that will almost certainly result in death if not treated immediately. While you are waiting for the vet to arrive, you can help the bird by providing heat. Heat will help the oviduct wall contract, but do not sit the bird directly on a heat mat because you do not want to burn or overheat her. It should be secured to the underside of the cage and only on one side to create a thermal gradient—one warm end and one cold.

Egg drop syndrome

Egg drop syndrome (EDS) is an infectious disease of laying hens caused by a virus and characterized by thin-shelled and shell-less eggs in otherwise healthy birds. The natural hosts for EDS are ducks and geese, but it has become a problem with chickens of all ages. The disease is most severe in broiler breeders and brown egg layer strains. Egg production is affected, with some deformed eggs being produced. Infected birds excrete the virus in their droppings, so hygiene is paramount to stop the spread of the disease. There is no treatment, but a vaccination at point-of-lay period will provide protection.

Egg peritonitis

This is another condition related to egg production, that can be fatal to your bird. Egg peritonitis is caused by yolk fluid leaking from the oviduct and ovaries into the abdominal cavity. The fluid builds up, causing a visible swelling of the abdomen. From there, the yolk can get into the bloodstream and poison your bird. Egg peritonitis can make a bird very sick and is difficult to treat. It is possible for the bird to make a full recovery if it is caught early. Treatment involves using a diuretic like Frusemide to clear away the fluid, and antibiotics to help the liver repair itself and to prevent further infection. The symptoms are similar to egg binding and you will probably notice the bird is panting and looking uncomfortable.

Fowl cholera

Fowl cholera is found in ducks, geese, chickens and turkeys and is caused by the bacterium *Pasteurella multocida*. It is an infection spread through contaminated water, soil, or feed and symptoms include excessive thirst, difficulty in breathing, loss of weight and a bluish tinge to the combs or wattles. It does not cause high mortality and can be treated with antibiotics in the drinking water. It is often carried by vermin so efforts should be made to deter them from the site.

Fowl pest (or Newcastle disease)

Fowl pest is a highly infectious disease caused by a paromyxovirus. Young chicks are particularly vulnerable as the disease strikes suddenly and apparently from nowhere. All poultry—but mostly chickens and turkeys—can be affected by this disease. The disease is usually fatal in chicks, but older birds seem to be able to recover and return to normal laying. Symptoms including wheezing and choking, followed by nervous disorders such as twitching or spasms. It is also accompanied by a characteristic green diarrhea. There is no cure for this disease, but vaccination in the web of the foot will prevent an infection breaking out.

Fowl pox

Fowl pox is a virus infection that affects chickens and turkeys and is transmitted by contact, mosquitoes or via their water and food. There are characteristic lesions or pox marks on the comb and around the beak and there may also be labored breathing in more severe cases. There is no cure for fowl pox, so prevention by vaccination is the only way to deal with the problem.

Fowl typhoid

Fowl typhoid is a bacterial infection (*Salmonella pullorum*) that can affect all types of fowl. In young chicks, it is characterized by weakness, drowsiness, anorexia, poor growth, pasting of the vent, and chalky white droppings, and death usually occurs in about 90 percent of cases. In older birds you will see signs of lethargy, huddling, wing droop, dyspnea, white droppings, and decreased egg production. Unless treated with antibiotics it can cause high levels of mortality. You need to bear in mind also that this can be carried via the eggs, so if you are intending to breed, you will need to have your birds tested first.

Frozen combs and wattles

This is a condition that sometimes affects poultry living in colder areas. It is usually caused by drinking, which makes the comb or wattles wet, leaving them vulnerable to frost bite. Chickens with larger combs can suffer badly, and if left unprotected their combs can actually freeze off, causing them pain and distress. Treatment is easy—unless your bird is difficult to catch—by rubbing the affected parts with a mixture of 5 parts Vaseline, 1 part glycerine, and 1 part turpentine every day, during exceptionally cold weather.

Gapeworms

If you see a bird repeatedly opening its beak and gaping without making any sound, then you should suspect that it is infected with gapeworms. Infection is caused by a round-worm called *Syngamus trachea*, which blocks the windpipe of the bird. The worms are transmitted via contaminated soil or food and travel into the lungs and trachea where they become embedded. It seems to affect chickens more than any other fowl, and leads to breathing and feeding difficulties, and the bird will become dull and lose its appetite. If you suspect gapeworms then isolate the bird and treat it with a poultry wormer, which is available from your vet. If you are free-ranging, the only long-term solution is to ensure regular rotation of the ground so that the parasites do not get a chance to build up.

Gizzard worm

The gizzard worm is a nematode worm parasite, *Amidostomum anseris*, that affects both ducks and geese. The gizzard becomes infected by fine, cotton-like worms, which attach themselves to the inner lining. It is usually a result of over-grazing the same piece of ground, so regular rotation is important. Older fowl seem to be able to resist a certain level of infestation, but young ones can quickly succumb. The first symptoms are when the gosling or duckling develops a slow, staggering gait and quickly becomes weak and starts to waste away.

This can be prevented by using a worm medicine in the drinking water.

Gumboro disease

Gumboro disease, also known as Infectious Bursal Disease (IBD), is a viral disease affecting young chickens. The target of this disease is the bursa of Fabricius, which is an important organ in a young chicken's developing immune system. It is a small, hardy virus that is resistant to a great range of temperatures, but can be killed by most disinfectants. The virus is rapidly spread by direct contact between birds and can survive for long periods of time on inanimate objects or contaminated feed, but does not spread through the air. Look out for signs of whitish or watery diarrhea that contains mucus, with very sticky litter and soiling of vent feathers. There are also signs of listlessness, dehydration and loss of appetite, but generally it only affects birds up to four months of age, as the bursa of Fabricius regresses after this period. There is no antibiotic agent to treat or control this disease so hygiene is important when handling young chicks.

Hairworms

Hairworms are parasites that cause damage to the lining of the intestine and can result in anaemia and pale egg yolks. A suitable poultry wormer should be given to destroy the hairworms.

Infectious anaemia

Infectious anaemia is transmitted via the egg and droppings, and is a virus that causes listlessness and reduced weight gain, and some mortalities in the initial stages. If the bird does recover, it should not be allowed to breed. There is no treatment, although antibiotics can be used to control secondary infections.

Infectious bronchitis

Infectious bronchitis can be a devastating respiratory disease to any poultry keeper as it affects chickens of all ages, types and breeds. It is caused by a virus that is known to have a high mutation rate, which enters the body by inhalation. The signs to look out for are sneezing, snicking, gasping and a watery discharge coming from the eyes and nostrils, as well as a drop in egg production. Some strains of this virus can infect the kidneys and cause permanent renal damage. It is also a virus that affects the quality of the eggs, and it is common for watery whites—a serious thinning of the thick albumen—and egg production drops drastically. There is no specific treatment, though antibiotics may aid in combating secondary bacterial infections. Increase room temperatures and provide good hygiene management.

Infectious laryngotracheitis (ILT)

This is a contagious respiratory disease characterized by gasping, neck extension, and conjunctivitis. It is caused by a virus (*herpes virus specie*) which may live for 8 to 10 days in the droppings and up to 70 days in carcasses. Although this disease is most frequently associated with chickens, it has also been found in pheasants, fowl, and turkeys, and it is believed wild birds may act as carriers. It is an airborne virus passed on when birds are in close contact such as those kept in cages or pens. The virus enters through the bird's eye, nose or mouth. The virus is also spread when the birds cough up the bloody mucus—litter and manure are also ideal transporting agents. Sunlight, heat, and drying appear to be the natural enemies of this virus and 1 percent Lysol or 3 percent Cresol will deactivate the virus in less than a minute. There are no treatments for ILT but antibiotics can be used to control secondary infections.

Leukosis

Leukosis is an infectious form of cancer caused by a virus that is transmitted from parent to offspring via the egg. Signs to look out for are depression, emaciation, loss of weight and enlargement of the abdomen, liver or bursa. Prevention is the best cure for leukosis so good hygiene is top of your list. Checking the antigen in the albumen is a basis for eradication.

Lice

A proliferation of parasites in a flock can result in the death of any or all of the birds so it is important to recognize the symptoms and act swiftly. Parasites are likely to be a problem where there is overcrowding, poor sanitation or an infected bird is introduced to your flock.

Lice (*Menopon gallinae*) appear as small, creamy brown insects that live on the body of the bird. They congregate mostly toward the rear end to lay their eggs. These will appear as chalky white blobs that stick to the base of the feathers. If you part the feathers you will be able to see the small, grayish parasites scurrying across the bird's skin. They live off blood, skin debris, or the roots of the feathers and there are more than 40 species. Louse powder is effective in controlling them and should be applied once every four days for two weeks. You must remember to treat the houses and perches as well, and it may be quicker to remove the birds and fumigate their house. Remember to put some louse powder in the dust bath as well. The irritation that lice cause to a bird makes it peck at itself causing sores and general depression.

Malabsorption syndrome

Malabsorption syndrome is typically recognized in broiler chicks between 1 and 3 weeks old. It is characterized by stunted growth, lack of pigmentation in the skin, feet or beak, slow feathering, broken or twisted feathers and undigested feed in the droppings. Diarrhea is common in the early phases. There is no effective treatment for severely affected birds, but sanitation and disinfection will reduce the spread. There are no vaccines available to prevent malabsorption syndrome, so make sure your chickens' feed is always dry and fresh.

Marek's disease

Marek's disease is another herpes virus disease that is transmitted via the egg. It generally affects chickens between 2 and 16 weeks of age, and leaves it open to other diseases as its immune system breaks down.

It is carried primarily by air within the poultry house in feather dander, dust, feces, and saliva. Infected birds carry the virus for life and are a source of infection to susceptible birds. Clinical signs are "gray eye," which is caused by tumors in the pupils and blindness, tumors of the liver, kidneys, spleen, gonads, pancreas, lungs, muscles or skin. If a bird develops tumors, it will gradually become emaciated and mortality is inevitable. There is no treatment for Marek's disease, so prevention is carried out by vaccination at the hatchery.

Pullorum

Pullorum disease, previously known as Bacillary White Diarrhea, is caused by *Salmonella pullorum*. It is an acute systemic disease of young chickens and poults. It is spread to the young via the egg and infected chicks spread the disease laterally in the hatchery. It is usually seen in chicks younger than 3 weeks old and the first indication is the high number of dead-in-shells chicks and deaths shortly after hatching. It is not easy to diagnose, but there may be the presence of white diarrhea and a pasting of the vent. Antibiotic treatment is not recommended as birds can become carriers. Control is usually by testing and culling of the infected birds.

Red Mite

The Red Mite is one of the most common mites affecting poultry and, although the parasites are actually gray in color they quickly turn red after a good gorge on blood. Little more than 1/50" in length, they spend most of their time hiding in crevices inside the chicken house, and wait for night to come and feed on the roosting birds. Red mite, if left untreated, can become a killer as the birds become listless, stop feeding and eventually fade away. Warning signs are pale combs and wattles, decreased appetite, no eggs and an unwillingness to go into the house at night. Inside the house you might notice a musty smell, small bugs that swarm all over you and make you itch, a white dust in the crevices and around the doors in the house, and obvious waxy clumps of red matter. Thorough cleaning of the house and surroundings is essential, dismantling, if possible, to expose any hidden surfaces. It is also a good idea to remove roof felting or insulation as the mites love to hide under it. The house can then be washed or sprayed with a red mite treatment. There is also a red mite powder that is very effective, but don't be disheartened if it doesn't work straight away as it works by abrading the shell and drying the mites.

Roundworms

Most birds are able to endure a certain level of roundworms (*Ascaridia* sp.), but under unhygienic conditions, roundworms can build up to an intolerable level. Found in the gut, these parasitic worms are about 2" in length, and if left untouched, can lead to anemia and pale egg yolks. Make sure the droppings do not build up and moving birds on to uncontaminated ground from time to time is very important. Many drugs are available from vets and they are easy to administer either in the birds' food or water, and regular treatment is advised for young birds. A badly infected bird will show loss of condition, poor growth, listlessness, diarrhea, and wasting (mainly in young birds).

Scaly leg

Scaly leg is an overgrowth of the scales of the bird's legs, caused by a nasty irritation by a little, burrowing mite. It bores its way through the skin and forms crusty deposits that force the scales outward. Chickens are the most common fowl to be affected, although turkeys, guinea fowl, quail, and pigeons can also get it. Birds usually peck at

their legs in an attempt to get at the irritation and, if the scales are dislodged, areas of their skin can bleed. This is not a condition to leave untreated, as the irritation makes the birds miserable. Any lesions on the legs and feet are then open to infection and these can be very difficult to treat as healing in this area is slow. Discomfort and lameness result and the bird should be isolated and treated without delay. The crusts can be removed easily with warm soapy water and an old toothbrush. You will need a preparation such as benzyl benzoate to kill the mites. The old cure was to apply an ointment of 1 part caraway to 5 parts vaseline, but paraffin is equally effective, as long as the treatment is continued until all the mites are dead. The proprietary medicine available from the vet is much quicker and more effective, so you might like to go down the more modern route. Before treating the birds, their housing should be thoroughly cleaned and the litter burned to prevent re-infection.

Tapeworms

It would be very difficult to stop poultry from getting tapeworms, as they get them from all kinds of insects. Insects carry an intermediate stage of the tapeworm, a larva that develops into the adult form when eaten by the chicken. It lives in the bird's intestine and the adult sheds segments of feces full of eggs to the outside world where they are picked up by the relevant host. They grow to about 4" in the gut, but are not a problem unless they are allowed to build up, so regularly worming is essential for the health of your flock.

Ticks

The fowl tick seems to affect turkeys more than chickens and can be a major problem if left untreated. A fully engorged tick can measure as much as 2/5" and cause much discomfort to the bird. Frequent inspection is necessary to combat ticks before their numbers increase to a harmful level. You need to treat the premises as well as the bird, because adult and nymphal ticks only stay on their hosts a short while before hiding in their surroundings. The litter, walls, floor and ceiling must be sprayed thoroughly, forcing spray into the cracks and behind nest boxes. Outdoor runs and feed troughs should be treated, too.

Vitamin deficiency

This is a quick guide to help you recognize the signs of vitamin deficiency in your flock.

Vitamin A
In young birds: Caseous eye (no odor), emaciation, weakness, ruffled feathers, lack of coordination, eyelids stuck together, watery discharge from throat, nostrils or eyes.
In adults: Egg production decreases.

Vitamin B₂
In young birds: Curled toes—the deficiency

is termed "curly toe paralysis"–poor growth, weakness and emaciation. Leg muscles are atrophied and flabby. The skin is dry and harsh.
In adults: Poor hatchability and egg production can occur. Dead embryos have "clubbed" down feathers. Pullets have severe dermatitis of the feet and shanks and incrustations on the corners of the mouth.

Vitamin D
In young birds: Soft brittle bones (rickets) and retarded growth.
In adults: Cage layer fatigue.

Vitamin E
Incoordination, tremors, rapid contractions and relaxation of the legs results in the name "crazy chick disease."

Vitamin K
Signs occur 2 to 3 weeks after the deficiency occurs. Hemorrhaging and anemia may be seen in young birds. It can cause increased embryonic mortality in breeders, and dead embryos can be hemorrhagic.

Wry neck

Wry neck is not a disease but a condition caused by brain or nerve damage in a young bird. The bird is deformed in that its neck is bent tautly over the body. It is best to put down any bird that is suffering from this condition.

ABNORMAL EGGS

Soft-shelled eggs

Caused by calcium deficiency, soft-shelled eggs can be a problem. The remedy is to feed oyster shell grit or baked, ground eggshells. Sudden shocks can cause the shell-secreting glands to malfunction, so if you live close to a rifle range, for example, your hens could be showing signs of stress.

Eggs with double yolks

Double yolks in chicken and duck eggs are fairly rare, and affect only about 1 in 1,000 commercial eggs. When an egg starts its journey inside the hen, the first thing formed is the ovum in the hen's ovary. This grows and the color changes from pale gray to the yellow we know as the color of the yolk. Once it reaches full size, the yolk sac breaks away (ovulation) and starts its journey down the oviduct where the albumen and the shell form around it. The process from ovulation to egg laying takes around 24 to 26 hours.

Normally, the next ovulation is triggered by the hen laying the egg, but occasionally things go wrong and two yolks are released at the same time. They travel down the oviduct together, being surrounded by one shell and giving us a double-yolker.

Eggs with blood spots

Blood spots in eggs are actually harmless, but unsightly. They vary from barely

distinguishable spots on the surface of the yolk to heavy blood contamination throughout the yolk. It is caused by blood vessels rupturing in the ovary or oviduct and could be caused by low levels of Vitamins A and K, or the result of shock or stress. There is evidence there is a hereditary tendency for this condition, so avoid breeding from such a hen.

Fertile eggs

Fertile eggs are quite common, but there is a general feeling that eggs for eating should always be infertile. There is no problem eating a fertile egg, which occurs only if there is a rooster among the hens.

Wind eggs

Wind eggs are small with no yolk. It is fairly common when a pullet first starts to lay. It is not important and can be ignored, unless the pullet continues to lay such eggs. Wind eggs can also occur in older hens if they are subject to sudden shock.

Green yolks

Acorns and the annual weed shepherd's purse can both have the effect of turning the yolks green. Check the pasture and rake regularly if necessary.

Raising Your
Own Chicks

SUITABLE BREEDING STOCK

No matter how many times you witness it, the moment when a chick emerges from its shell will always be magical, even more so to those who are new to keeping chickens. Having success with a small flock in your garden, the natural progression is to begin breeding your own chicks.

Now that you have decided you would like to raise your own chicks, your first task will be choose a suitable cockerel to run with your hens. If you are keeping your hens in an urban setting, then you will have to think carefully before buying a cockerel, because they can be noisy, which means they might be an unwelcome addition for your neighbors.

A heavy breed cockerel should have no more than eight hens at any time, and should be at least 10 months old before he is set to work. The lighter breeds can usually cope with 10 hens. Ideally you should choose one that is the same breed as your hens and you will need to check his appearance carefully to make sure he is healthy. He should have bright red wattles and comb, a glossy coat and a strutting, confident gait. He should not be related to any of your hens as this could cause deformities and genetic problems, and he should be removed at least twice a week to give him a rest. He will also need to have extra rations to help keep his strength up.

Depending on his performance, you will probably want to keep your cockerel for at least four to five years, as he will be at his prime. A particularly good cockerel can continue to mate until he is five or six, so be prepared for him to be around for a long time.

If you are buying a cockerel from a reputable breeder, he will have records of the bird's parentage. You should ask to see these because it is important you obtain a rooster is from a good strain, particularly one that is resistant to disease and non-aggressive personality.

LOOK AT THE FEET

It might seem bizarre to those of you who are not experienced with cockerels and mating, but the feet are a vital sign of a good performer. The feet of the cockerel must have smooth skin and straight toes, although this has no bearing on his actual fertility, it does affect the way he fertilizes the female. If the skin is smooth it will not be prone to infection as rough skin encourages muck to adhere to it. Straight toes are also vital in the cockerel's balance.

When the cockerel touches vent to vent with the female, balance is very important as this could mean that they do not connect properly and the female will not be fertilized. Follow this simple rule and your cockerel should be active until a ripe old age.

TRIMMING THE SPURS

As cockerels get older, the spurs at the back of their legs get longer. In some cases these can become very sharp and pointed and can cause damage to the sides of a hen as he mates with her. It is quite easy to miss this damage, as the hen's wings will cover the area. If the hen's skin becomes torn, she risks getting an infection.

The simple solution to this is to trim the spurs back to round the ends off—ideally they should be no longer than 1/2" in length. To trim the spurs you will need a sharp pair of cutters—large nail clippers are ideal for this job—and also a file for smoothing the edges. Care should be taken that you don't trim too much off, though. There is a blood vessel running down the middle of the spur, usually about three-quarters of the way along, and it needs to be avoided.

The easiest way to trim the spurs is to wrap the cockerel up in an old towel to stop him from wriggling around and help to make your job easier. Start by just trimming off the point, then keep cutting small pieces off until you see a tiny dot of blood appear

in the center of the spur. This is the blood vessel, which means you have to stop there. Then you can use the file to round the edges of the spurs off to make them neat.

Your cockerel will feel no pain as this is only the same as trimming our own finger or toenails.

ASSESSING ITS TEMPERAMENT

Another very important aspect of choosing a cockerel is its temperament, especially if you have young children around. You need to remember that a cockerel can jump a few feet off the ground and kick with his feet and spurs, as well as delivering a nasty peck. You may of course be buying a very young bird, which means his temperament can change during the breeding season, so constant assessment is vital. If it comes from a non-aggressive strain, then the chances are that your cockerel will be genetically calm.

Size does not play a role in aggression, as even some of the smallest cockerels can show nasty traits. If the breeder still has the father, then ask if you can see it and find out whether it is safe to go into a run with it. This will give you an idea of what your bird will grow up to be like. Just like other animal breeds, different chicken strains have different temperaments. Take the time to study the breeds before embarking on a breeding program and choose ones that are known to have a pleasant temperament.

Once a cockerel is used to his new surroundings and to having you around, you will quickly be able to assess his temperament. If the cockerel runs over to you when you go into the run, you can treat this as normal behavior. He will be attracted to you because you are his source of food. However, if he chases you after you leave the food, that can be seen as an aggressive act. A cockerel that chases after you like this is more likely to kick out than a cockerel who goes to his hens to tell them there is food available.

BREEDING STOCK

Hopefully you will have kept an accurate record of your hens' laying abilities and will know the best layers. Hens that have proved to be healthy and are not closely related to the cockerel will be the best choice. Once you have chosen your breeding stock, the birds should ideally be given a breeder diet that has the necessary levels of protein, minerals, and vitamins to ensure healthy chicks. If your hens show a deficiency in Vitamin B_2 (riboflavin), the chick may be born with curled toes and defective feathering. Where Vitamin D, calcium, and phosphorous are lacking, the new chick can show signs of rickets. This means that its legs will be rubbery and splayed and it will be unable to stand up. Also their beaks will not form properly and consequently are not strong enough to break their way out of the shell. Finally, a lack of Vitamin E can lead to what is known as "crazy chick" disease. The chick will not be able to coordinate its movements and because it can only look upward, it gives it the appearance of being crazy.

Hopefully, after your hen has been mated a few times, she will start to lay fertile eggs. For this egg to develop correctly, the hen has to maintain a body temperature of around 104°F. Once you have chosen the best eggs for incubation, you then have to decide whether you want to rely on a broody hen to sit on the eggs until they hatch, or whether you want to place them in an artificial incubator.

To give your chicks the best chance of survival, choose only eggs that show the best quality and texture of shell. Any that show ridges, chalky patches or are misshapen in any way should be discarded.

THE BROODY HEN

The broody hen is simply displaying the natural instinct to reproduce. The most recognizable sign of a broody hen is when she constantly sits on the nest. If you approach her she will give a loud, guttural squawk and fluff her feathers up until she is almost double her original size. If you attempt to remove her from the nest, she will remain fluffed up, walk around in circles clucking audibly, and then return as quickly as possible to the nest.

If you have decided to use a broody hen to incubate your eggs, it is advisable to move her away from the flock. The best place for your hen is in a broody coop that has a rat-proof floor and slats in the front that contain the hen if necessary, but allow the hatched chicks access in and out. These are easy to make and should be lined with good nesting material such as sawdust, wood shavings, or good quality hay or

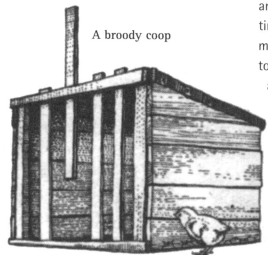

A broody coop

straw. Do not try to move the hen to its new quarters until her broodiness is well established, or she might become restless and there is a danger she could break the eggs. Try moving her at night rather than first thing in the morning, as this would be her normal roosting time and she won't be so restless. She should accept the eggs, even if they aren't ones she has laid, quite readily as her mothering instinct kicks in.

Provide both food and water, as well as a dust bath, within close proximity of the coop. She will probably leave the eggs only once a day to feed and take a little exercise and this will give you the opportunity to clean any droppings out of the nest and check that the eggs are in good condition. If the hen is reluctant to leave the nest, then you will need to lift her off once a day otherwise she will start to lose condition.

If you have ever seen a broody hen, you will notice that she frequently shuffles around on the nest, turning the eggs several times during the day. This is essential to make sure the embryo doesn't attach itself to the membranes on the downward side. It also ensures each side of the egg is kept warm, toxins are carried away, and the egg gets the right amount of oxygen.

It is also a good idea to sprinkle the eggs with warm water during the last three days of hatching, because this helps to keep the membranes that surround the embryo damp.

THE ARTIFICIAL INCUBATOR

If you do not have a broody hen available, then your second option is to use an artificial incubator. This can be a wise investment, and is an idea that goes back over 2,000 years. The Chinese used to hatch eggs in large, clay-brick ovens that were heated by burning wood. A good incubator should last you a long time and is worth the initial expense. Of course, if you are really enterprising, then you might like to make your own.

There are two types of incubator–the still-air or the fan-assisted. Still-air incubators are usually smaller and the air current is controlled by the manual opening and closing of vents. The fan-assisted ones use a fan to drive the air through the box.

Four crucial factors that influence the successful hatching of an egg:

• Temperature
• Humidity
• Position
• Movement

You will need to put your incubator in a place with a cool, constant temperature out of direct sunlight. You also need to make sure that it is somewhere where it won't get knocked easily. Although many people choose to site their incubators in an shed, the problem here is that the humidity can be quite high, which means the machine will struggle to maintain its levels. If you have a spare room that isn't used very often, this would be a perfect place for your incubator. The ideal temperature for the room is 75°F with a relative humidity of 60 percent.

Make sure you sanitize the incubator thoroughly before use. It should be allowed to run for at least 24 hours before putting any eggs in, so that the temperature and humidity are at the correct levels. Place water in the tray, a thermometer in the incubator so that the bulb is one inch above the floor and then close the incubator. You will probably need to adjust the thermostat so that the temperature stays between 99°F and 100°F. Do not allow the temperature to deviate beyond this, or you risk having a poor hatch. It is advisable to check the temperature at least twice a day.

You can check the humidity by using a hygrometer, and many modern incubators have these built in. Humidity should be set at 86°F and should not fluctuate more than 1°–otherwise the batch will fail–so make sure the water is always topped up. If the humidity drops too low during incubation, the contents of the egg can become thick and sticky, which means the chick will not be able to turn round, and the membranes will be too tough for the chick to break at the time of hatching.

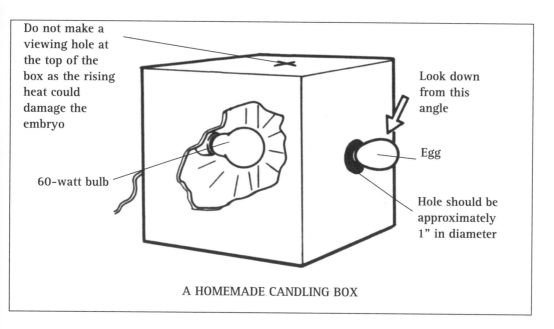

Do not make a viewing hole at the top of the box as the rising heat could damage the embryo

Look down from this angle

60-watt bulb

Egg

Hole should be approximately 1" in diameter

A HOMEMADE CANDLING BOX

TURNING THE EGGS

Many of the more expensive incubators will turn the eggs automatically, which means they will be moved every few hours. If you do have to turn them by hand it is a good idea to make a mark on each side, for ease of identification. They must be turned at least five times during a 24-hour period, but ideally it should be done once every hour if you have the time. Remember, though, the eggs should not be turned at all during the last three days of incubation.

CANDLING

Not every egg that your bird has laid will have been fertilized, so by looking more closely you can find out whether there is a baby bird developing inside. This process is known as candling. This should be carried out whether you are incubating them naturally or in an artificial incubator. Candling literally means holding the egg up to a bright light to see what is going on inside. It is very easy to make your own candler, simply by placing a 60-watt bulb in a box with a hole cut in the opposite side. If you use the box in a dark room, you can hold the egg up against the hole and the light from the bulb will penetrate the eggshell. If the egg is fertilized it will show up as a dark red spot with veins radiating out in every direction.

Make sure you have washed your hands thoroughly before handling the eggs, or alternatively wear lightweight rubber gloves. Candling should be carried out before incubation to check for hairline cracks and other defects and seven days after being placed in the incubator to check for any infertile ones.

HATCHING

Chicken eggs take 21 days to hatch, but the incubation period is slightly different depending on the species of poultry. The following are the approximate number of days you should allow for incubation:

Chicken	21 days
Duck	28 days
Turkey	28 days
Muscovy duck	between 33 and 35 days
Goose	between 29 and 31 days
Guinea fowl	between 26 and 28 days

On the nineteenth day—for chickens that is—you should be able to hear the chicks trying to break the shell; this is called "pipping." You do not need to turn the eggs now, because the chicks are getting ready to hatch. Avoid trying to help the chicks out of the shell: they are quite capable of doing it themselves, however tempting it might be. If you interfere, you risk rupturing the blood vessels, so only assist if you are aware there are real problems. If all the other eggs have hatched and dried off, and there is one still struggling to come out after some period of time, you can bathe the shell in a little warm water, which will help the shell to break. Make sure that you do not allow any water to get into the chick's nostrils because you could risk drowning it. Don't be surprised if some of your chicks do not hatch or die shortly after hatching. There are many reasons for this and it is almost impossible to predict these problems with any certainty.

Once the chicks hatch, they will quickly get to their feet and their down feathers will start to dry. They should be left for 24 hours before you move them to a brooder. It is not necessary to provide food and water at this stage, because they still have remnants of the yolk inside them.

The following day move the new chicks to a brooder that has a warming infrared lamp to stop them getting chilled. Now you can give them some chick crumbs and water to welcome them into their new world. You might need to encourage them to eat and drink in the early stages, and this can be done by gently dipping their beaks into the food and water. Alternatively, you can imitate the mother hen by dropping some chick crumbs on the floor, which should encourage them to eat.

Hygiene is very important at this stage and make sure you do not allow a buildup of droppings or you will increase the risk of disease. Also you need to make sure your brooder is in an area that is safe from rats and mice.

Once your chicks are able to do without the artificial heat, they should be given their own run with some grass to encourage foraging. It is not a good idea to mix them with the older birds at this stage, because of the risk of disease. For the same reason, do not put them on ground that has previously been used by other birds, but make sure it is a fresh patch.

INTRODUCING DAY-OLD CHICKS TO A BROODY HEN

If you would like to take the more natural approach after your chicks have hatched, you can always introduce them to a broody hen. She will need to have been sitting for at least two weeks, if you want to increase the chances of her accepting the brood. Of course she still may not accept them, but if she does you will have saved yourself the trouble of having to brood them yourself.

Introduce the chicks gently, one by one. You will need to make sure she does not see you handling the chicks, so make sure you introduce them from behind. If she is already sitting on eggs, take these out of the nest and then replace each one with a chick. A large hen will be able to accommodate as many as 14 chicks. If you hear her responding to their chirping by doing a gentle clucking sound and then spreading herself protectively over them, then you have every chance that she has accepted the new brood. Do not take this for granted though, check every couple of hours to make sure she hasn't abandoned them at a later stage.

THE BABYSITTER

If your broody hen successfully hatched a batch of eggs on her own, you can leave the chicks with their foster mother in the broody coop until they are at least one week old. Provide some chick crumbs and a little light bedding, such as sawdust, which shouldn't be any more than 3/4" to 1" deep. The mother hen will quickly teach her new chicks how to feed and drink. It is your job to keep the chicks dry and free from drafts, and the hen will provide all the warmth they need. You will need to shut them in at night, so for a while your routine will be much the same as that of your adult chickens.

By three weeks, the chicks will be old enough to be allowed out in a run with their mother. They will need to be injected before they can finally be introduced to your original flock.

SEXING YOUR CHICKS

The problem you will now be faced with is that many of your chicks will be males, and unless you are a big operation and plan to continue breeding, they are usually surplus to requirements. The problem is that sexing baby chicks is very difficult, in fact, almost impossible. The only accurate way is to wait until they start showing some of the male characteristics—the larger comb, tail feathers and the more upright stance. Their voices will also change from the gentle chirp to a more manly squawk. Unless you have a breed such as the Cambar, which produces identifiable sexes at hatching, just enjoy watching them grow up and then decide what you are going to do with them.

INCUBATION PROBLEMS

This section finishes with a few problems you could encounter if raising your own chicks and the possible causes.

Eggs do not develop
Infertile eggs or left too long before incubating.

Eggs clear when candled
Cracked or damaged eggs, possibly diseased.

Eggs gone bad
Disinfect incubator before use and dip eggs in sanitant. Check that the parents' stock is fertile.

Blood ring in shell
Temperature fluctuations—check thermostat. Possible bacterial infection. Possible viral infection. Ensure the parents are healthy and free of inheritable diseases by having their blood tested.

Chicks hatching too early
Temperature too high—check thermostat.

Weak chicks
Temperature too high—check thermostat. Deficiency of essential amino acids—make sure you feed parents supplements.

Deformed chicks
Too much inbreeding, hereditary diseases.

Beak or splayed leg deformities
Insufficient calcium, phosphorous, or Vitamin D in parents' diet.

Curly toe paralysis
Vitamin B_2 deficiency in parents' diet. Allow grass ranging or feed supplement of chopped boiled egg, Marmite, yeast, or ground-up yeast tablets.

Clubbed ends to down feathers
Vitamin B_2 deficiency in parents' diet. Feed supplement as above.

"Crazy chick" disease
Vitamin E deficiency in parents' diet. Too much corn given instead of wheat. Feed supplement as above.

Developed chicks dead in shell
Levels of temperature and humidity too high at critical hatching time. Deformities of the beak may have prevented the chick from pecking its way out of the shell. This could be the result of inbreeding, inadequate parental feeding or a hereditary disease.

Generally low hatching rate
Any of the above reasons. Possible lack of Vitamin B_{12} or shortage of trace elements in the parents' diet. Feed properly and give a supplement of ground-up multi-vitamin tablets.

The Egg

NATURAL FOOD PACKAGE

Nature has been good to us by providing a ready-made, natural food package in the form of an egg. It is rich in nutrients, contains many essential vitamins and minerals and, in addition, it is totally versatile.

Breakfast, brunch, lunch, or dinner, the egg can be adapted to suit any meal. Fried, boiled, poached, scrambled, or simply added to other ingredients, this versatile food can provide us with all the essential amino acids that we need. The protein can be found in both the white and the yolk and with their relatively low content of saturated fat, eggs can be a valuable part of a healthy diet. Eggs also contain the majority of the recognized vitamins with the exception of Vitamin C. It contains all of the B vitamins, vitamins A, D, and E, and iodine, which is important in the development of the hormones that control our thyroid glands. Added to all this goodness are the benefits of phosphorus, which aids in the development of our bones, as well as selenium, zinc, and iron.

Some people may be concerned about the amount of cholesterol that an egg contains, but this fat-like substance is still necessary to maintain the function of many of our body cells. It helps keep us supple and our skin in good condition, so eaten in moderation cholesterol can be beneficial.

Eggs come in different sizes and colors and whether the shell is brown or white, the nutritional value is exactly the same. The color of the yolk is determined by the diet of the hen. Hens fed a diet rich in corn generally produce darker yolks, while wheat-fed hens produce paler yolks. It is the yolk of the egg that contains the majority of the vitamins, while the white carries most of the protein.

All eggs sold are graded for quality and freshness. Only Grade A or AA eggs reach store shelves and because many people believe brown eggs are better for you, they are prized for the commercial market.

Most people believe that when they buy eggs, the freshness is determined by the sell-by date on the box. This is not quite correct. It is more accurately described by the date when the egg was actually laid and how it has been stored. If the egg has been properly handled and stored before it reaches the shops, then it will be relatively fresh. However, an egg refrigerated for a week will never taste the same as one you collected that morning.

HOW LONG DO EGGS KEEP?

A newly collected egg will stay fresh for about 4 to 5 weeks if refrigerated, without any significant loss in quality. You will soon know if you have a bad egg—the smell will hit you as soon as you crack the shell.

HOW TO TEST IF AN EGG IS FRESH

If you are in any doubt as to the freshness of an egg, there is a simple method of testing it. Simply fill a bowl with cold water and lower the egg into it. If the egg is fresh it will sink straight away, if it is stale it will float on the surface. The reason for this is because the air cell in a fresh egg is exceptionally small. As the egg starts to age, more air enters the egg through the shell and when immersed in water the enlarged air cell makes the egg float and stand upright. The general rule is if the egg floats right to the surface of the bowl, throw it away as it is not fit for human consumption.

The other way to test for freshness is to break the egg on to a flat plate. If it is fresh the yolk will remain round and relatively firm, with the white staying close to the yolk. If the yolk flattens and the white spreads across the plate, this is a fair indication that the egg is getting past its best.

COLLECTING YOUR EGGS

You should collect your eggs as regularly as possible, causing your hens the least amount of stress. Unless you have the specially designed rollaway nest boxes, eggs left in nests are at risk of getting trampled on and broken, and probably will become soiled with droppings. There are things you can do to minimize the chance of collecting soiled eggs, and it all comes down to good house management. You will need to make sure you regularly change the material in the nest boxes and if there are any broken eggs, remove them promptly to discourage egg eating.

It is advisable to collect your eggs early, as soon as you open the pop-hole to let your hens out in the morning. Look again in the evening before you shut your hens away for the night, as many birds like to actually roost on the edges, or even in, the nest boxes, which means there will be mess on your eggs.

Traditionally, a wicker basket was used to collect the eggs, but any container that is designed to carry eggs safely is fine.

SHOULD I CLEAN THE EGGS?

This is a matter of choice and some people do prefer to clean their eggs before storing them. If you are one of these people, you might like to consider that unwashed eggs have a natural bloom, which is antibacterial in itself. Dunking them in cold water is not a good idea, as the pores on the surface of the shell can actually draw the bacteria inside. You can dry clean your eggs, which will leave the majority of the bloom intact. First, sanitize an abrasive sponge and simply rub off any dirt from the surface of the egg. If, however, the eggs are too soiled to dry clean, then the best method is to stand your eggs in a wire basket or sieve and spray them with warm water. Wipe them dry afterward with a piece of kitchen towel.

Before storing your eggs in the fridge, mark each carton with the date they were collected, so you know which to use first.

CAN I SELL MY EGGS?

If you have a surplus of eggs and would like to sell some, you will not need to register with any official body as long as you follow these simple rules:

• You only sell eggs that were collected on your premises.

• You only sell your eggs at your own gate or farm shop, door-to-door sales, or at a farmer's market.

• They are not graded and sold by sizes.

• They are very fresh and unwashed.

•For backyard chicken operations, pasteurization is not necessary. The U.S. Department of Agriculture (USDA) only requires eggs to be pasteurized before sale if they have been broken and are used in a processed product.

• You do not need organic certification from the USDA or certification from other agencies unless you specifically want to label your eggs as "organic." It is against USDA regulations to use the term "organic" on any food product unless it has been certified under the National Organic Program standards.

• You will need to check with your state department of agriculture to ensure you are following local health and sanitation requirements for selling eggs.

If you have decided to sell your surplus eggs, you will need to advertise the fact to your neighbors or indeed any passers-by. The best way is to put up a sign large enough to be read from the road in a position where it is easy to see. The best way is to make a sign on your computer keeping it simple such as EGGS FOR SALE. Laminate the sign to keep out the rain. You might also like to tell your prospective customers how to buy the eggs, either by trusting them to put money in a box or asking them to knock at the house. You might also like to make a second sign saying something like SOLD OUT or NOT LAYING TODAY, so that the person does not have a wasted journey.

EGG SIZES

Egg sizes have changed over recent years in terms of selling terminology. In the United

States, eggs are sold as:

Jumbo: 2.5 ounces
Extra Large: 2.25 ounces
Large: 2 ounces
Medium: 1.75 ounces
Small: 1.5 ounces
Peewee: 1.25 ounces

In the United Kingdom, eggs are sold in Small, Medium, Large, and Very Large.

Very Large: 2.5 ounces or more.
Large: between 2.2 and 2.5 ounces.
Medium: between 1.9 and 2.2 ounces.
Small: 1.9 ounces or under.

WAYS TO PRESERVE EGGS

With modern refrigeration, preserving eggs is not a necessity as it was in the past, but our ancestors didn't like to waste anything and devised various ways of keeping food from spoiling. The first two are probably methods that are still in use today, but the remainder are really only included for your interest.

Freezing

It is possible to freeze eggs for around three months, but you will need to remove the shells first, otherwise they will burst. The most convenient way of freezing eggs is to break the eggs into an ice-cube tray, separating the whites from the yolks. Add a little salt to those yolks that will be used in savory recipes and a little sugar for those for use in cakes or desserts. **Remember to mark which is which so you don't mix them up!** The salt and sugar stops the yolks from becoming sticky when you defrost them. Once the squares are frozen you can remove them and package them in bags—two white squares and one yellow will be the equivalent to one whole egg. Alternatively you can use your extra eggs in sponge cakes and then freeze these, which keep well until you have an unexpected guest.

Pickling

The practice of pickling eggs has been around for many years, and was a great way of preserving eggs before the advent of the modern refrigerator. You can often see a jar of pickled eggs standing on the counter at a delicatessen or an old traditional pub or bar. Many people still like to preserve eggs this way and use them on picnics or in packed lunches. There are many different recipes to choose from but the one included here is the standard one that was used in old inns.

Ingredients

12 hard boiled eggs
1 finely chopped chilli pepper
1 quart of malt vinegar
10 black peppercorns
10 whole cloves
3 cinnamon sticks
2 tsp allspice

Method

1. Hard boil the eggs and remove the shells. Cool the eggs and then place them in a large, clean glass preserving jar.

2. Place the vinegar and spices in a saucepan and bring to the boil. Reduce the heat and simmer for about 10 minutes.

3. Remove from the heat and leave to cool to room temperature.

4. Strain the liquid through a sieve or muslin and then pour over the eggs, making sure they are completely covered.

5. Seal the jar and leave in a cool, dark place for at least two weeks before eating. Eggs can be stored in this way for two to three months.

Waterglass

This is another traditional method of storing eggs, but is probably not used much today. Traditionally, the eggs were kept in an earthenware pot with a lid, but any high-density food-quality container will do. You will need to make sure all the eggs are clean and free from any cracks or blemishes. The waterglass solution is one part sodium silicate to nine parts water. The eggs need to be covered completely by the solution, but you can keep adding new eggs each day until the container is full. It was said that eggs would remain fresh for six months by using the waterglass method, but it would still be advisable to smell the eggs after cracking to make sure they are still fresh. It is possible that some with hairline cracks get missed and put into the solution.

Other traditional methods of preserving

You are welcome to try any of the following but none of them seem to keep eggs fresh any longer than the domestic refrigerator.

- Dry cheap cooking salt in the oven and then pack the eggs in an earthenware crock with salt above and below. They will remain fresh for up to three months.

- Rub clean, fresh eggs with lard, butter or paraffin, prolonging their life by one month.

- Paint clean, fresh eggs with a solution of equal parts of gum arabic and water.

- Place eggs in their shells in a solution of brine, which is said to preserve them for a month.

Showing

WORTHY OF A PRIZE

Even if you only started out keeping chickens for their eggs, most poultry keepers at one time or another have bred or bought a particularly impressive looking bird that they felt was worthy of a prize. Many people will do nothing about it, but it is worth mentioning a few pointers if you should decide to show your birds.

Although this section is not going into much detail regarding showing your chickens, it is intended to give guidance to those people who do not know where to start.

If you wish to go down this route, then your bird will need to be a purebred recognized by the American Poultry Association. It doesn't matter how beautiful your hybrid bird might be, it cannot be accepted for any show classes. If you would like to learn more about the individual breeds and their suitability for the show ring, your local poultry and agricultural shows are a great place to start. There will a variety of birds on show and many breeders who will be only too pleased to share their knowledge with you.

Once you have decided on a particular breed, joining a relevant society will keep you informed of all shows and will give you details of what you need to do. They can also give you guidance on what is expected of your bird—the ideal feathering, stance,

coloring etc. There is a system of points allocated for each different characteristic, and these add up to 100. Each bird is scored according to its dominant characteristics and the higher the score the better.

When starting out, it will be difficult to find a bird that is at the top of its class, as breeders tend to keep the best for themselves. If you are really keen on showing it might be up to you to breed that perfect specimen. Ideally, you should buy your hen and cockerel from two different sources so there is no risk that they come from the same line. Some breeds are now so rare that it is possible they are all related anyway, but you should take every caution to avoid close ancestry.

Although some people might question why people would want to show, the simple answer is that apart from the obvious enjoyment, it is also a good advertisement for declining breeds. Hopefully it will encourage more people to breed from declining strains so they do not become extinct. With more than 220 breeds of chicken now extinct, and another 100 on the critical list, it is now up to us to make sure other breeds are not lost for ever.

Before embarking on your first show it is a good idea to visit one and see what is expected of you and your chicken. You will be able to see how the judges handle and inspect the birds and what type of carriers people use to transport their birds.

If you choose a bird you would like to show, this should be given an outdoor run and separate house from the rest of the flock. Because this bird will spend much of its time in a small show cage, the least you can do is to reward it with some pleasures when it is at home.

The feeding of a showbird follows the same rules as birds used for breeding purposes, ensuring they have vitamin and mineral supplements to keep them in prime condition.

Make sure you treat your show birds regularly for red mite and lice and you should also take precautions against scaly-leg mite, because these would all affect the overall condition and appearance of your bird. You would also not be welcome at a show if you were going to spread these pests to other birds.

You will also need to make sure the bird's claws and beak are trimmed neatly, but be careful not to overtrim.

TRAINING YOUR SHOWBIRD

Because it is essential that your showbird gets used to being handled, it is handy to have a space allocated indoors where it can get used to people. It needs to learn that it doesn't have to panic when it comes to being judged.

All the time you are handling your bird make sure you are talking to it in a calm manner. In this way, it will quickly learn to be at ease with its handler. You also need to teach the bird that the showcage is not scary, so consequently put it in and out of the cage, remembering to talk to it all the time and always acting in a calm manner. If you become stressed, your bird will quickly pick up on your emotions and react negatively. When taking the bird out of the cage, open the door slowly and carefully insert one hand underneath the bird, while confining the wings with the other hand. Make sure you do not make any jerky movements and you should find you have no problems.

Once the bird is used to handling and getting in and out of the cage, you will need to teach it how to stand still. This can be achieved by standing it on a flat surface and stroking its back feathers gently with a bamboo cane. Certain breeds need to adopt certain stances, so this is something you will need to read up about. For example, the Indian Game is required to stand with its legs wide apart. You can either do this with your bamboo cane or with your hands, whichever you prefer.

ENTRIES

When you have decided which shows you would like to enter, you will need to check when the closing dates are for entries. Make sure you do not leave your entry until the last minute because late entries are never accepted. Keep a record of the shows you have entered so that you do not become confused and double book. Poultry magazines list various shows and addresses of people you can write to obtain schedules and show details.

PREPARING FOR THE SHOW

Now it is down to you to make sure your bird looks its best. If your chicken is white- or cream-colored, you might need to give it a wash with a mild baby shampoo and warm water. This is gentle and will not sting if it gets in the bird's eyes, but this should be avoided if possible. Every bird will need its feet and legs cleaned thoroughly in warm water before showing to remove any excrement or dirt. This can be done with mild shampoo again in a bowl of clean water, using an old toothbrush to help remove the caked-on dirt.

The easiest way to wash a bird is to have two plastic bowls full of warm water, one for washing with baby shampoo added and one clean for rinsing. Hold the bird firmly so it cannot flap its wings and then immerse the bird in the water up to its head. Gradually work the soap into its plumage and then clean the face with a small piece of sponge. Gently squeeze out the surplus lather and then transfer the bird into the bowl containing the clean water.

Gently towel the bird dry, making sure not to drag any of the feathers roughly. Smooth the feathers back into place and then put the bird into a warm place to dry. If you have a bird with a calm temperament, it might be possible to finish drying it off using a hair dryer on the coolest setting, which will also help dry the feathers fall back in a natural position. If the handler is careful and calm, your bird should thoroughly enjoy the whole experience of bathing.

Bathing should be carried out at least one week before the show to allow enough time for the natural oils to build back up in the feathers. To help get a glossy sheen to the feathers, they can be rubbed using a piece of silk, but make sure you follow the natural line of the plumage.

You might find many of the dark breeds do not need bathing, and you can normally remove any dust or grit by brushing the feathers gently.

Once you feel your bird is ready, place it in a nice clean, dry run away from other birds and give it plenty of food and water.

TRAVELING

No bird should travel for more than 12 hours without food and water. The bird's welfare should be your prime concern and should be kept in mind when choosing the type of carrier for transporting your bird. There are specialist suppliers of show cages and traveling boxes. Many people opt for cardboard boxes for traveling because they are disposable and will not need to be cleaned afterward. They come in a variety of sizes and as long as they have ventilation holes and a secure place to put food and water, they should be ideal.

Make sure the traveling box is secured firmly in place as you do not want it to slide around and cause the bird any stress. When you arrive at the showground, present your entry and then put your bird in its showcase. It is a good idea to get there early so your bird has time to settle and you can do last-minute grooming. If necessary, apply oil, petroleum jelly, or hand cream to the comb, wattles, and legs and rub a silk handkerchief over its plumage. Hopefully, its feathers should be in tip-top condition from its feeding regime in previous months.

Provide a fixed waterer in the cage, but food is not normally fed just prior to showing. You can take some grain with you to give to the bird when it is all over.

THE FINAL JUDGING

When the judging is over make sure your bird has some food and its water container is filled. Your birds will have to stay on the site until you are given a specific leave time. Make the most of this time and speak to other exhibitors and stewards and learn as much as you can before embarking on your second show. When the winners are announced you could also ask why these particular birds were chosen, which will provide you with guidance for the future.

BACK HOME

When you return home, your bird deserves a little pampering. Dust it with flea powder as a precautionary measure and do not let it join the rest of the flock until you are certain it has not bought anything nasty home with it. If it is showing any signs of stress, keep it isolated and give it a bit more special care and attention. Paying extra attention at this stage means you will be able to show your chicken again.

A GUIDE TO WHAT A JUDGE LOOKS FOR

When showing chickens there are a number of factors that the judges will take into consideration. They will look at the bird as a whole, not just individual features.

There are two categories—production and purebred. Hens in the production classes will be judged on their past and current laying condition. Roosters will be judged on their physical condition and activity. You need to select a bird on its body conformation and also its sexual maturity.

DESIRABLE CHARACTERISTICS

- **Head**—should be broad and flat on top as opposed to round, with a nice gap between the eyes.
- **Face**—should be smooth and free of wrinkles. The skin should be soft and a nice large comb that is bright in color. The eyes should be large and bright, with nice round pupils.
- **Body**—needs to be well-developed and broad.
- **Feathers**—should be in good condition with no plumage missing.
- **Feet and toes**—the birds should be well balanced with nicely shaped feet and toes.
- **Sexual maturity**—Hens should be in full egg production. If she is in full production, her comb and wattles should be large, soft, red, and waxy. The pubic bones should be wide apart and flexible.

The abdomen should be soft and pliable, and the vent large, moist, and free of any pigment. Roosters should be alert and active and show a strutting gait.

UNDESIRABLE CHARACTERISTICS

- **Tail**—split, wry, or squirrel tail, or entire absence of main tail feathers.
- **Wings**—split, slipped, or clipped.
- **Back**—hunched or crooked.
- **Beak**—rubbery or deformed.
- **Feathers**—any twisted feathers in primary, secondary, tail, or sickles.
- **Weight**—any bird that is excessively underweight according to its breed type.
- **Comb**—any defects or foreign characteristics to the specific breed.
- **Head and adjuncts**—any abnormal coloring that is not associated with a specific breed. Incorrect eye coloring or positioning.
- **Legs and toes**—Any signs of knock knees or bowlegs. Absence of spurs on roosters. Abnormal number of toes. Color of shanks, toes, or feet foreign to a specific breed of chicken.
- **Color**—any definitive variation in color from the breed characteristics—e.g., red or yellow in a pure black variety.
- **General health**—showing any signs of poor condition, disease, pest, or deformity.

Ducks, Geese, and Other Poultry

DUCKS

Ducks are perfect for the back garden but differ from chickens because they require access to water. Not all breeds need large ponds; some domestic ducks will be content with a child's wading pool.

Ducks are not as prone to disease as chickens, and provided they are fed the correct diet and kept safe from predators, they can make great family pets. Be prepared for a duck to be around for a long time though—they can live as long as 20 years. Some breeds are prolific layers, so if you enjoy the flavor of their eggs, you will be in for a treat. They also act as great "guard ducks" because they will make a loud quacking sound whenever anyone is close, particularly the Call duck, which, as its name suggests, can be very noisy.

Ducks can be a lot messier than chickens and can be fairly destructive if allowed to roam free in a vegetable garden. They particularly love lettuces, peas, and young brassicas, so you might want to put some fencing up to keep them out. They love to investigate and will search for insects and slugs in your herbaceous borders and on the lawn; although they won't do much damage, they might trample a few delicate plants down with their webbed feet.

Provided you give ducks access to some sort of water container large enough for them to swim in, they will be happy. This may only be a child's wading pool with rigid sides or a large feed bowl, or plastic pond liner—they are not fussy. Water is essential to their well-being because they need to regularly preen their feathers. By dipping in water, the duck can activate its preen (*uropygial*) gland, which is situated near the base of its tail. This tiny gland contains an oil which the duck uses to coat its feathers in order to make the outer ones waterproof. The duck picks up the oil using its head and beak and smears it over its body to prevent it from becoming waterlogged. Underneath the oily outer feathers are the soft downy ones that keep the duck warm. Preening also helps to remove parasites and scales that cover newly sprouting feathers, so you might often see a duck with its head buried deep in its body cleaning itself up.

The duck also has special feet, which are adapted to a life in water. These are webbed, meaning they have skin that stretches between the toes, so the feet act as paddles when it is swimming. It is this feature that gives the duck its characteristic waddle when out of water. Ducks can even swim in icy water because their feet have no nerves or blood vessels, which means they cannot feel the cold or become affected by icy conditions.

The duck's mouth is usually referred to as a bill or beak, which is characteristically broad and flat, but varies from breed to breed. The bill has notches all along the edge; these are called *lamellae*, which act as a grip to stop food slipping off the otherwise smooth surface. The bill varies considerably depending on the duck's natural feeding habits. For example, a shoveller has a really broad beak that is used to sift food out of the silt at the bottom of rivers and ponds. Dabbling ducks feed on the surface, with short, broad beaks, searching under the surface of the water without submerging totally. They look for plants, seeds, and other small insects, with the lamellae allowing the water to filter out the side of the beaks leaving the food inside. Diving ducks have long narrow beaks with more pronounced lamellae that allow them to hold the fish that are the staple of their diet. These ducks submerge themselves while searching for food.

Because ducks are so reliant on their feathers, they need to replace old and worn out ones from time to time and this usually takes place in late summer and early spring. Ducks lose the majority of their feathers during a seasonal molt, and this renders the birds flightless for a short period of time putting them at greater risk from predators. The molting process can take up to two weeks, and you will notice the replacement feathers are dull and lacking any luster for a while. In the wild, a duck would seek a sheltered place where food is in abundance, to help them get through this period. Ducks rely on a high proportion of protein in their diet to maintain their plumage in good condition, because the feathers themselves are made up of a high percentage of protein—almost one-third of the total body's quota. To allow for this, extra protein should be fed during this period.

A number of drakes will live quite happily together, but you should never have more than one drake running with female ducks because it can cause friction.

CHOOSING A DUCK

If you only have a small area in which to keep ducks, it would be advisable to choose one of the bantam or miniature breeds because they are far more manageable for the beginner. They are small and light, do not make a lot of mess and will be quite happy with a small pond or large basin. You will not have too many eggs, either. You will have to remember, though, that all of the miniature breeds are good flyers so they will either need to be kept in a covered pen, or their wings will have to be clipped. It is also advisable to keep them in pairs, as a single female could decide she wants to go off and find a mate.

Bantams and miniatures

Unlike chickens, in duck breeds the bantams and miniatures are all simply smaller versions of the larger breeds, and include—Silver Appleyard Miniature, Silver Bantam, Black East Indian, and the Miniature Crested. There is also the Call duck, which should really be put in a class of its own as it is quite unique and has been developed from dwarf genes. This endearing small duck was formerly called the "Decoy" as it was often used to attract wild ducks into an area because of its loud quack. It has a short, compact body with a round face and short bill. Call ducks are easy to tame and make great family pets as they are amusing to watch with their inquisitive behavior. They come in a variety of colors and are the perfect breed for the newcomer to duck keeping.

The Miniature Silver Appleyard is the bantam version of the much larger Silver Appleyard, originally created in Britain by Reginald Appleyard during the 1940s. They are an attractive duck with an irridescent green head color and distinct body markings. Drakes have green bills while the ducks have yellow. Although much smaller than the regular version, their eggs are of a similar size, laying from March to June. As with most miniature breeds Appleyards can fly well, so netting the pen or clipping their wings is essential if you don't want to lose them.

Crested ducks are comical little fowl, with a fluffy pom-pom on the top of their heads, which makes them almost appear as if they are wearing a bonnet. They are a relatively new breed, having only been accepted as a breed standard in Britain in 1997, and consequently are not so easy to obtain. The crest is a mutation and does not appear the same from duck to duck, with the best specimens usually kept for showing. You need to be aware that this crest can become damaged during mating and that any ducklings produced will not all necessarily have the characteristic crest. The breed is great for gardens as it loves to forage. It can lay up to 100 eggs in a year. Crested ducks can be of any color. The crests can vary considerably from bird to bird. The crest is a growth of fatty material that covers a hole in the skull—a result of a cranial hernia. Because this mutation is attractive, it has been encouraged in breeding, but in the wild a bird with this mutation would probably not survive. Crested ducks are not ideal for beginners.

The oldest breed of bantam is the Black East Indian, a duck that was developed in the United States. The best specimens are striking in appearance, with their black bill, eyes, and legs showing an almost beetle-green sheen. A peculiarity to this breed are the early eggs, which sometimes appear with an almost black hue to them. This does not affect the quality of the egg and can be scraped off quite easily. As the season progresses the eggs gradually fade to a more normal, dull white.

LARGER DOMESTIC DUCKS

Aylesbury

This is one of the best-known ducks and has been around for more than 150 years. Like the majority of ducks, the Aylesbury was derived from the Mallard during the early part of the eighteenth century. It is a heavy, white breed, generally bred for its meat rather than its egg-laying capability, which can vary drastically from 30 to 100 eggs a year. The Aylesbury is one of the greediest birds and seems to live to eat. Large and stocky, it needs plenty of space, too.

Muscovy

This South American purebred is the only duck not derived from Mallard stock. In the wild, the Muscovy coloring is black and white, but domestication has produced a variety of colors. Muscovies have strong, sharp claws designed for grabbing tree branches, as their favorite roost is high in trees. They are not good swimmers; their oil glands are not highly developed as in other ducks, so their wing and tail feathers often become ragged and untidy in appearance.

However, they are a strong breed and are not prone to illness. The only real downfall to keeping a Muscovy—apart from its love of flying—is its passion for small rodents such as mice and baby rats. Make sure you do not keep them near your child's pet guinea pig or rabbit, because they could be on the menu! It has the nicest character of all the domestic ducks and is relatively silent, so ideal for someone who has neighbors close by. The male produces a low hissing sound, while the female has a habit of chirping to her eggs as they hatch so they will recognize the sound when she wants to raise an alarm call. The Muscovy breeds exceptionally well, and not only will it raise its own young but will happily act as a foster mother to other eggs as well.

Buff Orpington

The Buff Orpington was first introduced in the late 1800s, but was not officially recognized as a true breed until 1914. A dual-purpose bird, it can lay as many as 220 eggs a year. The Buff Orpington is a very easy breed to raise. It gains body weight rapidly, making it an ideal table bird. It has a long, broad body, with an oval head, medium length bill and a long curved neck.

Khaki Campbell

This is one of the best breeds to choose for egg production in many parts of the world. If properly housed and fed, it is capable of producing more than 300 eggs a year. Needless to say, you will have to find out about the family genetics of your stock before buying to ensure it comes from a good line of layers. Campbells are alert and sprightly and love to forage, spending a lot of their time looking for slugs, snails, and worms with which to supplement their diet. They love water and do not mind how it comes as long as there is a sufficient supply for them to carry out preening.

Pekin

Pekins are a dual-purpose breed imported into the United Kingdom and the United States in 1873. A prolific layer, the Pekin has been bred to discourage broodiness, so if you want to breed Pekins, you will need to incubate your eggs. Pekins are active birds and do not do well in small pens, preferring to be allowed to search in long grass and dabble around in a bit of mud. Their feathers tend to be soft and fluffy, lose quality when the weather is particularly wet. Because they have a limited amount of oil to protect their plumage, clean bedding is essential. Feather quality can be improved by adding extra vitamins to the bird's diet. Pekins are large, robust birds with the characteristic wobbly walk. Disney's Donald Duck is said to be based on the breed.

Indian Runner

Before the Khaki Campbell knocked it off the top spot, the Indian Runner was one of Europe's most widely kept breeds. It was their value as egg layers that brought them fame in the United Kingdom, and they are today a favored breed among duck lovers. Their short thigh bones give them an unusual gait, similar to that of a penguin. They come in a variety of colors, with the range still expanding—Black Chocolate and Blue are the latest to choose from. They are quiet birds and flightless, which means they need to be protected well from predators, so an enclosed, secure run is essential.

Cayuga

The Cayuga duck breed was developed from a pair of wild black ducks that a miller in Duchess County, New York, caught on his millpond in 1809. The birds were pinioned to prevent them from flying away, and afterward promptly settled into life on the miller's pond.

Some of the descendants of these birds were brought to the Finger Lakes region of New York in 1840. These ducks became popular in northern New York and were named Cayuga after the native people of that area. By 1874, the Cayuga duck was accepted into the American Poultry Association's Standard of Perfection.

A Cayuga's bill is black with occasional olive tips and the feet are black to dusky black that may acquire orange shading later in life. The plumage of the Cayuga is uniformly greenish black and may become mottled with white as they mature. Their meat is of fine quality, but the carcass can be difficult to clean because of their dark feathering. Some resolve this problem by skinning the ducks rather than plucking.

The Cayuga is a prolific duck and can lay 100-150 eggs per year. Eggs are initially black in color, but as the season progresses egg color lightens to light gray, and then to white by the end of the season. They are known for their flavorful meat, ideal in dishes such as duck confit.

The Cayuga, to this day, is recognized as one of the hardiest of the domestic ducks and is easily tamed if hand-raised. They tolerate the harsh winters of the northeast and can produce many offspring. The Cayuga averages 7-8 pounds and has the ability to obtain much of its diet from foraging, when given appropriate areas to explore for food. ALBC's 2000 census of domestic waterfowl in North America found 1,013 breeding Cayuga.

Welsh Harlequin

Originating from the Khaki Campbells, these medium-sized ducks are docile, inquisitive and good layers. The best strains can produce as many as 300 eggs a year. They rarely fly so they need to be well protected. The males have a greenish-black head with reddish shoulders frosted with white. The females have an almost golden appearance, with brownish green or bronze bands on their wings. The breed loves to forage and enjoys space as long as the area is safe.

Rouen

Another ancestor of the Mallard, this breed has similar markings but is larger and more brightly colored. It was developed in France in 1874 and even today is considered to be the superior bird for meat. Rouens are calm, love to forage and are unlikely to fly. The laying rate varies considerably, with the best strains laying 100 to 150 eggs per year.

Swedish

Because tradition held that blue colored ducks were "exceptionally hardy, superior meat producers, and difficult for predators to see," this type duck had been popular in Europe for centuries. As early as 1835, the foundation stock of the blue Swedish duck was being raised by farmers in Pomerania, which at that time was part of the Kingdom of Sweden, but today straddles northeast Germany and northwest Poland. Swedish ducks were imported into North America in 1884 and included in the American Standard of Perfection in 1904. Since then, they have been raised in modest numbers as general-purpose farm ducks as well as for pets, decoration, and exhibition.

The Swedish is medium-sized, weighing between 6 1/2 and 8 pounds. The American Standard specifies the outer two or three wing flight feathers must be white but this difficult specification has discouraged many breeders, and is unimportant for general use. While Blue is the only Standard variety, Swedish ducks also come in Black, Silver, and Splashed color patterns.

The Swedish is a "utility breed which matures fairly slowly and provides well-flavored meat." In confinement they do not thrive as well. Swedish will lay 100 to 150 white, green, or blue tinted eggs yearly. Typically they have calm temperaments and make fine pets.

SYSTEMS FOR KEEPING DUCKS

The importance of water in keeping ducks has already been stressed. If you do not have a pond, an old bath or sink in the ground will do, but whatever you use you will need to make sure it is cleaned and refilled frequently, otherwise it will quickly stagnate. Ducklings are prone to chilling and should not be allowed access to water until they are eight weeks old. If you have a pond there could also be a problem with rats, which can attack small ducklings.

If you are not worried about the damage, ducks can be kept free-range, although it is advisable to make sure they are housed at night, or face the risk of predators.

Where land is limited, as in a garden, you might have to confine your ducks to a run. The ground will become muddy quickly, so consider laying concrete on at least half the run. It might be a good idea to close off any grassed areas on very wet days, which will minimize damage. Ducks do very well on concrete provided it is smooth; any abrasive surface is bad for their feet.

Although ducks can survive without housing, if you want the best production from your ducks, it is a necessity. Ducks love to sleep somewhere dry and free from drafts. They also need to get out of the hot sun. The housing must be strong enough to keep predators out, and windows should be covered in wire, not glass, placed high up in the house. Ducks are easily spooked, so it is not advisable to have a window at a level where they can see out. They will need a minimum of one square yard per duck, and obviously far more in the run.

If the door does not open at floor level, you will need to provide a ramp, because ducks can't climb or jump up. You do not need to provide nest boxes; ducks happily lay on the floor, if there is clean bedding, usually straw, so they can make their own nest. Doors need to be fairly wide; ducks routinely leave the house en masse, and can sustain leg injuries due to trampling.

Wood is the best material for your duck house. Dimensions will depend on how many ducks you intend to keep. You do not need to provide perches. Be certain you have easy access for cleaning.

Many predators love ducks, so your fencing will need to be high and have an overhang or an electrified top. To prevent predators from digging underneath, make sure you bury the wire into the ground.

FEEDING

Free-range ducks with access to an established pond will instinctively find their own food in the form of grass, insects, slugs, water fleas and small fish. They could survive on this diet, as wild ducks do, but a duck will only lay to its full egg potential if it is regularly fed on foodstuffs that contain the right balance of nutrients.

You can do the feed-on-demand system whereby you use a hopper containing duck pellets, allowing the ducks to help themselves whenever they feel like it.

It is advisable to place waterers well away from the hopper, as ducks have a habit of dunking food in water.

You can also feed kitchen scraps as an addition to the diet, and plenty of chopped green leaves each day. If eggs are your priority then use layer's mash or pellets. If you are fattening ducks for the table, then rearer's or broiler's pellets are best.

EGGS

In the past there have been a number of scares regarding salmonella in duck eggs, and the reaction by the public caused a drastic drop in the number of eggs sold.

Any eggs that are laid on damp, dirty straw or on the edge of a muddy pond are at risk of infection, because the shells are porous, but this would apply to chickens' eggs as well. As long as the eggs are laid on clean, dry straw or any other type of bedding used in a duck house, there is no reason to suspect infection. If you want to clean eggs, you can use a piece of sandpaper and rub off the worst bits. You can immerse them in warm water (114°F), but only for a couple of minutes otherwise the shells will absorb the moisture. If you add sanitizing agents to the water, the eggs need not be rinsed afterward, which means the protective bloom will remain intact.

Ducks tend to lay their eggs during the night or early in the morning, so it is advisable to keep them locked up until about 10 a.m. and hopefully by that time they will have finished laying. Pick up the eggs as soon as the ducks leave the house, and check again throughout the day.

Duck eggs can be used for all the same things as hens' eggs, except they are larger and you won't need as many. If fresh, they do not have the strong flavor some people dislike, but you might notice the white is more rubbery than a hen's egg, so you might prefer to just keep them for cooking.

THE ONSET OF LAYING

It is common for first-year layers to show no signs they are about to lay. When ducks reach sexual maturity they seem to develop strange behaviors—the characteristic head bobbing that takes place between the duck and the drake. If you notice it, egg laying will probably start within the next couple of weeks. If you are intending to breed ducks, you will need one drake for every four to six ducks.

THE BROODY DUCK

Broody ducks behave in much the same manner as a broody chicken, in that she fluffs up her feathers when you approach and she will be more inclined to peck. She will normally leave the nest once a day to feed and will take a short swim before returning to her eggs. This swim maintains the humidity of the eggs throughout their incubation. If the duck does not have access to water, sprinkle the eggs with water regularly to stop the membrane from drying out. Feed the duck daily at the same time.

Broody ducks appear agitated and will make a distinct nest lined with their own feathers. If your duck makes a nest in an unsuitable spot (that is, one where predators can reach it), you may have to move it or build some type of protection around it. Moving a nest is rarely successful.

When you first approach her she will make a hissing sound that you probably haven't heard before. She will fluff herself up and try and look as fierce as possible. When she feels she has laid a sufficient clutch, she will start sitting, turning, and controlling the humidity as a part of her inbuilt broody state. Once she has hatched a couple of eggs, she may get bored and leave the remainder of the clutch unprotected. You may have to take the rest away and finish their incubation artificially.

There are occasions when a duck may turn on her own chicks, in which case you will need to remove them to a safe place and keep them warm with an infrared lamp.

INCUBATION

Much of the information regarding hatching and incubating chicken eggs applies to ducks. Duck eggs take 28 days to hatch, but the main difference is the humidity has to be higher, so make sure the water reservoir if always topped off if you are using an incubator. After a week, handle the eggs to make sure they are fertile.

If you are incubating the eggs using a broody duck, you will need to make sure you choose a breed known for broodiness; some ducks make terrible mothers. It is possible to use a hen to hatch duck eggs, but be cautious. Ducklings raised by a hen will not be waterproof until they are at least one month old, and so cannot go into water or they risk drowning.

CARING FOR DUCKLINGS

Ducklings are easy to raise and it is common for the whole clutch to survive. If you do have a runt, you might see it throwing its head back along the back of its neck. This is an indication the duckling is about to die and there is nothing you can do about it.

If ducklings are not being raised naturally by the duck, you will need to keep them warm, ideally at a temperature of 70°F to 90°F for the first few days. After four to five days the temperature can be gradually reduced by a few degrees a day, until they are two weeks old, at which time they will be ready to be hardened off.

Chick or broiler crumbs are the best food for young ducklings, and can be left for them in a shallow container. Water should be available at all times, but should be in an enclosed drinker for the first week, rather than a open dish.

Ducklings are much easier to sex than hens' chicks, and can be sexed even at one day old. It is easy, but you will need to make sure you do not cause the duckling any unnecessary pain. Hold the duckling firmly, but gently, to expose the vent. With the finger and thumb of the other hand, push back the vent gently on either side so that it is open and extended. In a male bird, the penis can be seen as a small organ that is attached to the inside top of the vent.

As ducks grow, they make different sounds—the duck a definite "quack"; the drake a sort of croaky whistle. Drakes tend to have curly tail feathers.

AILMENTS

Ducks are hardy birds and if kept correctly should remain free of problems. The type of problems you might encounter are:

Worms—roundworms, gizzard worms, or gape worms, which, although harmless in small numbers, in a large infestation would eventually cause the bird to lose condition. De-worm your ducks regularly.

Parasites—these are not such a problem on ducks as they are on chickens, but it is still worth taking precautions by thoroughly cleaning the duck house on a regular basis. Check regularly for leeches and ticks, and also watch out for maggots around the vent area on birds with thick plumage.

Lameness—probably the biggest problem you will encounter if you keep ducks. The webs on ducks' feet damage easily if they tread on something sharp. An untreated foot wound easily turns into bumblefoot.

Breathing problems—these can be largely avoided if the duck house is kept clean, well ventilated, and dry. Moldy bedding or food can leave unpleasant spores.

Crop binding—this is when the crop becomes impacted. If this happens the duck will need immediate veterinary treatment.

Slipped wing—you may notice the primary feathers on a young bird turning outward, or dropping. The usual cause of this is when ducklings are fed on a diet that is too rich in protein, meaning they grow too fast for their bodily development.

If you suspect one of your ducks is unwell, then isolate the bird immediately, keep it warm, provide it with food and water and then call for the assistance of an avian vet.

GEESE

These birds are not only a long term commitment—they can live for as long as 30 years—and require a lot of room, so don't consider them if you are short of space. They can also be quite vocal. If you have neighbors who prefer peace and quiet, geese are not for you.

Having just given you the negatives about keeping geese, there are still plenty of positive aspects, and if you have plenty of ground with grass available, they are first class grazers and foragers. Geese are good guards, because they honk loudly whenever anyone or anything visits.

In the past, geese were often kept for their feathers—a valuable filling for mattresses and pillows. The larger tail feathers were also used as writing quills, and for this reason abbeys and monasteries often kept flocks of geese. It is a trade that seems to have died out, but there is no reason you couldn't bring the tradition back and fill your cushions, quilts, or pillows with beautiful, soft downy goose feathers.

Geese do not take to confinement because they need to graze on grass, but even free-range geese will need a secure barn at night to keep them safe from predators. Even a bird the size of a goose is not able to protect itself against a determined fox. The goose house only needs to be a simple garden shed, as long as it is strong enough to keep out predators. It needs to be dry, with good ventilation, to avoid causing respiratory problems.

Orchards make perfect places to keep geese, as the trees offer shelter from excessive sun. Geese also like to forage for windfall apples and are great at clearing pastures of weeds. Pastures will have to be checked for any poisonous plants, such as deadly nightshade, laburnum, or yew, and that there are no sharp objects lurking in the long grass. Once the grass starts to lose its nutritional value in late summer, you will need to supplement the birds' feed.

Geese are waterfowl but do not require water in the same way that ducks do. They like to spend most of their time on dry land, although they will appreciate access to water. It does not need to be as large as a pond, a large bucket deep enough for them to immerse their heads will keep them happy.

If the area is safe from predators, a three-sided shelter is adequate for geese. Line the shelter with clean straw and make sure the roof has an overhang so that rainwater does not run back into the shelter. You will not need nest boxes or perches, but the amount of space is important because geese tend to rest in pairs once they have chosen a partner.

The structure can be quite simple: straw bales for the walls and a roof constructed from overlapping pieces of corrugated galvanised iron attached to wooden planks. This is a cheap way of giving geese shelter and keeping them out of the elements.

A basic outdoor shelter is fine for geese as long as the area is free from predators

CHOOSING YOUR GEESE

If you are thinking of buying geese, the minimum number you should have is two. Unlike chickens and ducks, geese mate for life and they do not thrive well when on their own. Try to choose a breed known to be non-aggressive, as geese do tend to have a reputation for fierceness. The breed and how you raise your geese will be the determining factors as to their temperament. You will need to watch the gander when his goose is sitting on eggs, because he will become protective and could easily chase you away.

Chinese

It is believed the wild Graylag goose was the ancestor of most domestic geese—with the exception of the African and the Chinese goose. All geese make excellent guards but the Chinese is by far the best, if you are looking for one that will act as an elegant lookout. It is one of the most popular breeds of domestic geese, and is characterized by a large knob on the top of its bill. The Chinese come in brown, white, or gray and are renowned for their loud voices, which are unsuitable if you have neighbors close by. Ideally you want one that is noisy when anything unusual is around, but is happy to be handled by its owner, so you need to be careful how you rear and handle it from the outset. Some Chinese geese are excellent layers and can produce as many as 80 eggs a year. Their light body weight and small feet mean they can be less messy than some of the other breeds, but they are not always ideal with small children.

Roman

The Roman goose is one of the smaller breeds and was introduced into the United Kingdom from Italy at the beginning of the twentieth century. Romans are usually white, but some birds appear with gray markings down their back. They are stubby little birds and prolific breeders, with blue eyes, reddish-orange feet and a pink-colored bill. Many Roman geese have tufts or crests although these are not as common in the United States. A friendly, tactile bird, it is ideal for beginners. In folklore it was this type of goose that raised the alarm when Rome was under threat of invasion by the Gauls.

Embden

This is the largest of the utility breeds, and is usually kept for its meat. It is pure white with a bright orange bill and legs, and clear, blue eyes. It has a large body and an almost swan-like neck and is renowned for being hardy. The female will start laying early in the year, and can produce between 30 and 40 eggs. Embdens are expert foragers and very adept at feeding themselves, but if kept in an enclosure they will quickly eat the area bald. Be careful if you keep these geese in an orchard because they are likely to strip the trees of their bark.

Steinbacher

This breed is a relatively new addition to domestic waterfowl standards, introduced from Germany in the 1980s. It is a fairly small bird with an unusual pale lavender-blue plumage. Although originally bred as a fighting goose, the Steinbacher is recognized today for its placid temperament. It is probably one of the easiest breeds to tame, which makes it the ideal choice for anyone with a young family. Steinbachers are confident with people and it is possible to keep ganders together in the same flock without any risk of fighting.

Toulouse

The Toulouse group of geese is one of the largest breeds and was originally identified by its large dewlap—a loose flap of skin hanging underneath the neck. However, the utility Toulouse goose lacks this because it has been interbred. Its originated in France, where it was a considered to be a superior bird for the table. The Toulouse is also one of the main breeds used to make *foie gras* (goose liver served as a *pâté*)—a practice many poultry keepers object to vehemently. It is also kept for goose fat, because of its ability to put on large amounts of weight. Despite its size, the Toulouse does well in confined spaces, because it is not adept at foraging. Toulouse goslings are slow to mature, but if crossed with an Embden gander they do grow much quicker. Gray is the primary color of the Toulouse, with deep furrows on the sides of the neck, an orange bill and orange-red legs. The geese are very fertile and good egg layers, but the sheer size of them might put you off keeping them at home.

Pilgrim

These medium-weight geese got their name from the Pilgrim Fathers, who introduced the breed into the United States. The breed is unique because you can tell the sex of the gosling from the color of its plumage—the gander is white and the goose light gray. Young females tend to start out with a gray face, but the feathers go white with age and form "spectacles" around the eyes. The Pilgrim is common in the west of England as a farmyard goose because it is extremely self-sufficient, a good grazer and has a very strong tendency to flock. Most strains of the breed are exceptionally tame.

African

Despite their name these geese did not originate in Africa. They are one of the heavy breeds that came from China and reached Britain in the reign of Queen Victoria as the Hong Kong goose. They are impressive birds, standing as tall as 3 feet, but are one of the leanest for their size. Mature birds have a large knob above their bills; the knob and bill are black in the Brown form and orange in the White. The African has a large dewlap, similar to the Toulouse. It lays moderately well.

Huoyan

This breed originates from China and is similar to the Chinese goose, but with a much lighter body weight. Prolific layers, Huoyans can produce as many as 200 eggs a year. They are predominantly white with orange shanks and beaks, although some strains do come in other feather colors. They are known for their resistance to cold and will make the best of what foraging materials are available.

FEEDING

The most economic way of keeping geese is to rely on the nutrients of grass. Young goslings can be left to graze as soon as new grass appears in the spring and this, along with water, will provide them with nutrients they need until the autumn when grass begins to decline. Traditionally, they would be slaughtered in winter for the Christmas table, but as a smallholder you will probably want to keep your geese longer and will need to supplement their feed.

Goslings do very well on a diet of proprietary chick crumbs and water for the first few weeks of their life, but they will need something green to graze on as well. Geese are born with the instinct to peck at grass, and even after a couple of days they will need something to peck at otherwise they could start picking at each other's down feathers or pieces of straw. Of course this only applies to goslings that are being artificially reared, as any that are roaming with their mother will have access to grazing. Chopped chives and onion tops are welcome additions to their diet, or a clean piece of ungrazed turf, which will satisfy their pecking instinct. Goslings should not

This should be fed to them twice a day. The greens can be any leafy vegetable such as cabbage, celery, herbs, lettuce, or dandelion leaves.

As winter approaches, a good mixture if you are fattening them for the table is:

1 part wheat
1 part barley
1 part oats

This can be fed either dry or soaked, twice a day. Don't forget the addition of some greens to complete the winter diet.

Over winter, when no grazing at all is available, your geese will need to be given enough nutrients to keep them in good health and to fight the cold. Wheat and oats are a good combination in the proportion of 3 parts wheat to 1 part oats. Also feed them the outer leaves of winter vegetables, such as brassicas; apple peelings make an extra treat. Feed your geese twice a day and keep an eye on their water supply to make sure it isn't frozen.

be put outside to graze until they are at least three weeks old, and even then they will need to be brought in at night until their plumage develops enough for them to withstand the change in temperature.

Young geese who have regular access to pasture do not need additional food. If you only have limited grazing available, your geese will need other rations and then it can start getting expensive. The best all-round food is:

1 part oats
3 parts chopped greens
2 parts wheat

BREEDING

For breeding purposes the heavier breeds like the Embden or the Toulouse will need one gander for three geese in every set or family. For the lighter breeds, one gander to four or five geese is fine. If you are thinking of keeping more than one set, it is fine to leave them to graze together, but you will need to provide separate housing for each family.

Unlike chickens, geese have not been specifically bred for laying, and therefore produce comparatively few eggs and then only during their natural breeding season. The lighter varieties are known to lay more eggs, so you might like to start with one of these breeds if you want to raise goslings.

The abdomen of the goose will drop when she is about to lay. You can look out for this, but it is not a totally reliable sign, because many older geese have dropped abdomens already. Far better to watch the behavior of the gander, who will show signs of aggression when his female is about to lay and become very protective. This is a time to keep small children out of his way. Make sure the geese are restricted to an area where they are safe and secure and cannot do any harm.

Egg laying starts at the end of the winter and, as each egg is laid, the goose will cover it over with straw or whatever other nesting material she can find. She will lay one egg per day until she has a clutch of approximately 20 eggs, at which time she will start to sit. She may lay her eggs in a totally unsuitable place even if you have provided her with a lovely, dry nesting box. There is no point in trying to move them; it is more sensible to construct a shelter around your goose's chosen spot and leave her to get on with it.

Most domestic geese are good sitters and will not neglect their eggs during the incubation period of 30 days. The gander is on guard all the time; as soon as the goose lets out a warning honk, he will rush up to the intruder with his wings flapping and warn them off.

Occasionally two geese will try to share the same nest. This is not always convenient because the eggs are not usually laid at the same time which means they are going through different stages of incubation. There is little you can do about this, so you may have to accept that not all the clutch will hatch.

If your goose is not a good sitter, you can use a broody hen. However, the eggs will be too large and heavy for her to turn, so you will need to do this for her several times a day. It is easiest to make a mark on the egg on one side, so you do not get confused. The eggs will need to be sprinkled with water occasionally to stop the internal membranes from drying up. Two eggs are usually enough for one hen to raise.

If you want to raise the goslings in an incubator, you will need to treat them the same way as chicken eggs, but the humidity will need to be set slightly higher.

RAISING HER YOUNG

Geese are fairly good mothers, but not nearly as protective as most broody hens. Rats can be a major problem and will kill young goslings in a matter of minutes, so you will need to be alert. If you are not sure about their safety it is probably advisable to remove the young from their mother and put them in a safe, warm place until they are big enough to look after themselves. Provide the young brood with some gosling crumbs and drinking water.

Do not put young goslings out to graze before they are three weeks old. They should not have access to swimming water either, as they are not waterproof until they are fully feathered. When you do eventually put them out to graze, make sure it is on fresh grass that has not already been grazed by adults. Adults can withstand a certain amount of parasites, such as gizzard worms, but they would quickly kill a young goose.

If you are lucky enough to have an excess of eggs, then they can be used in cooking much the same way as chicken and duck eggs. They make wonderful omelettes and, of course, you don't need many because they are so large.

HEALTH

As long as you keep your geese clean, well fed with plenty of fresh grazing, and safe from predators, you should not have too many problems with their health. Many predators, including foxes, enjoy geese, and will snatch a goose when she is sitting on her eggs, if given the chance. If you know there are foxes in the area, then make sure your sitting goose is in a fox-proof place. Large adult geese who are grazing can usually look after themselves, but if you do not put up adequate fencing you chance losing a few.

A healthy goose will be alert, have nice bright eyes, feed well and will be happy to splash and preen in water. If your goose is not well, it will appear dull and lifeless, perhaps with a discharge from its nostrils. It may not be feeding well. Look for signs of mess around the vent, or feather loss. If you suspect any of your geese are not in good health, isolate them immediately to a clean, dry pen and seek veterinary advice.

Lameness can be a problem in geese, the same way as in ducks, so it is important to make sure there is nothing sharp in their run or pasture.

If you notice a discharge from the eyes, this could be caused by an imbalanced diet or insufficient clean water for the bird to bathe in. Make sure its diet has the correct nutrients, and provide clean water. Ask your avian vet for some eye drops or ointment, which should quickly clear the problem.

Parasites can be another problem, particularly in young geese. You may notice that they are off their food and have diarrhea, which can either be caused by a bacteria from unclean living conditions, or worms that are living in the gut, such as Coccidiosis. Young birds can die quite quickly from digestive problems, so make sure your birds are regularly wormed and that their grazing area is changed regularly.

Another parasite that can attack geese is the fluke (or trematode), but this is only normally when a bird has access to a natural lake or pond. If ingested, the fluke can invade every part of the bird's body. The only practical solution is to remove the birds from the source of the infection.

In extreme weather, geese can suffer from frostbite, especially the breeds that have knobs above their beaks.

As explained earlier, vermin can cause many problems to someone keeping geese, so it is imperative that you keep on top of the problem. They are initially attracted by the goose's food, and their presence can quickly spread disease. Take all the preventative steps possible to avoid vermin, and if you intend to use poison make sure you speak to a specialist first to ensure it will not be harmful to your birds. The best way of preventing the presence of vermin is to clear up any spilled food immediately, keep food in vermin-proof containers and block up any holes in the fences or housing where you think they might be coming in. If you do see a place they are coming in, it is a good idea to place traps.

TURKEYS

Think of turkeys and Christmas immediately springs to mind. Admittedly not the prettiest of birds, turkeys are actually quite easy to keep although they are not suitable for a small back garden or anyone with limited space.

Frozen turkeys are relatively cheap to buy from supermarkets, but anyone who is concerned about where their poultry comes from and the conditions in which they were raised might like to try keeping a few free-range birds. It is now possible to buy maxi, midi or even mini turkeys, so you have quite a choice depending on the amount of space you have available. If you have an area of around 45 square yards, then you have enough room to keep one male (tom) and one female (hen).

Turkeys can become quite tame and will quickly realize who is providing their daily food. They do have a tendency to wander, though, so wing clipping is advisable if you want to make sure they keep to a designated area. Turkeys can be a great joy to keep and, despite their strange appearance, you will quickly come to treat them as pets.

CHOOSING A TURKEY

Wild turkeys were hunted almost to extinction after the arrival of colonists in the Americas. People quickly realized their benefits as food, and so domestication and selective breeding became paramount to save the birds. Heavier, meatier birds were gradually developed in the United States and Europe, and in the mid-nineteenth century the famous Bronze turkey came into being. From this old strain, newer breeds were introduced such as the Broad-Breasted Bronze and the Broad-Breasted White, both of which are still popular today.

The Broad-Breasted White is the dominant turkey on the market today, but breeders are now making an effort to reintroduce some of the Heritage breeds, which are prized for their beautiful plumage. These breeds include the Narrangansett, White Holland, Standard Bronze, Bourbon Red, Jersey Buff, Slate and Black Spanish.

Many broad-breasted varieties have been so interbred that they are not able to mate naturally due to their size. Commercially they are bred by artificial insemination, so if you are looking for a breeding pair, choose one of the lighter breeds.

Narragansett

This variety of turkey was first introduced in Narragansett Bay in Rhode Island, and eventually became the foundation of the turkey industry in New England. The breed has a calm disposition and shows good broody instincts, making it ideal for breeding. It produces excellent meat quality, too. The Narragansett comes in black, gray, tan and white color patterns, not dissimilar to the original Bronze. This bird is ideal to keep on a small, family farm.

Bronze

This turkey gets its name from its unusual coloring, which is an almost metallic greeny-bronze. It comes in two types—the Broad-Breasted and the Standard—both of which are in decline. They are calm and easy to handle and stately in appearance, but more breeders are required to bring this magnificent turkey back into fashion.

Bourbon Red

This is aptly named "Red" for the rich, chestnut color of its plumage. It was a very important commercial variety in the 1930s and 1940s, but quickly lost favor to the broad-breasted varieties despite its heavy breast and richly-flavored meat. Thanks to the efforts of conservationists, though, the breed is now making a comeback. Bourbon Reds are handsome birds, with red wattles, black beards and white tail and flight feathers.

White Holland

This is another breed under threat, having been an important commercial bird raised in the early 1900s. It is showy in appearance, with white feathers and a red, blueish tinged head. The beard is black, the beak is pink, and the throat and wattles are pinkish-white. Over time many of the true white varieties have been lumped under one title—British White in the United Kingdom and Large White in the United States.

Norfolk Black

This was one of the favored eating birds in Britain in the 1700s. Black turkeys tend to have a smaller breast than the White varieties, but their meat has a full and gamey flavor. Black turkeys in general are closer to the original wild strain and tend to produce more eggs than other breeds.

Slate and Blue

The Slates are often referred to as Blues or Blue Slates, and are related to the Blacks. The Slate is an ashy blue with specks of black scattered across the feathers. The Blue is more of a solid, gray-blue, the hens being lighter than the toms. The hens and toms have red to bluish-white wattles, heads and throats, horn-colored beaks, brown eyes and black beards regardless of their body color. They are a medium-sized turkey that breeds reasonably well, but they are quite rare so can be difficult to find.

Royal Palm

Royal Palms are one of the smaller breeds of turkey and have consequently been raised for their ornamental value rather than their meat. If you have a young family, or a limited amount of space, this could well be the turkey for you. These birds can be highly strung but also very adept at foraging for themselves. The Royal Palm has the same basic pattern as the Narragansett, and is most common in black and white. The hens make good mothers and the toms are known to be non-aggressive.

Beltsville Small White

In the 1930s, there was a demand for a smaller turkey, one that would answer consumer demands for a bird that would fit in the meat compartment of a regular refrigerator and small oven. The result was the Beltsville Small White. Its success was short-lived, unfortunately, and by the 1970s, it was nearly extinct. It did have the advantage over its heavier relatives of having good reproductive qualities, including the ability to mate naturally. In recent years there has been a revival of interest in this turkey and efforts to build up stock are underway. The plumage is white, with a black beard, a horn-colored beak and dark brown eyes.

Jersey Buff

As the name suggests, the Jersey Buff has a rich reddish-buff coloring, with white tail feathers which generally have a buff bar across them. The birds have black beards and hazel eyes, and both toms and hens are the same color. They are calm birds and easy to work with, making them ideal for families with children and limited space. The hens are good egg producers and are able to mate naturally, which is a great advantage to those who want to continue the strain.

Broad-Breasted

The Broad-Breasted is not recognized as a true breed and comes in White and Bronze standards. It is the mostly widely-kept domesticated turkey, because it produces a lot of breast meat. Many turkey keepers will argue that due to their fast development and factory farming much of the original flavor has been lost. They are a large breed and unable to mate naturally; reproduction is by artificial insemination. They are popular as a table bird because of their lack of dark pin feathers which many believe spoil the appearance of the meat.

HOUSING

Turkeys are happiest when they are kept free-range, and due to their hardiness, this normally causes no problems. It is not a good idea to graze them on land where other poultry have been, because of the increased risk of disease. They do not prosper on damp, badly-drained land; the disease Blackhead thrives in these conditions and can have a devastating effect on flocks. Dry, chalky soil is the best, particularly where trees can provide natural shade.

Turkeys are tree perchers by nature, but this activity has been curtailed considerably by breeding heavyweights that do not have the same agility. If you are only keeping a couple of birds, you could use the fold method used to keep chickens. This is where the birds are confined to one area and then moved to a new location as the ground becomes overworked.

If you are allowing your turkeys to free-range you must still provide them with some form of shelter, bearing in mind they are still subject to the usual predators. A dry shed or building will be fine, as long as there is adequate ventilation and a thick layer of clean litter such as woodshavings is put down on the floor. Do not keep too many birds together in a confined space or you will greatly increase the risk of infection. Ventilation is important as turkeys can suffer from respiratory problems, and dusty, damp litter can cause sinusitis. Like any poultry keeping, good hygienic management of the flock and housing is essential. If you clean the house regularly using a safe disinfectant, your birds should stay free of disease.

FEEDING

Turkeys do not do well unless they are fed correctly. Turkey poults require more protein than chicks and will not thrive if fed on chick crumbs. You can buy special turkey starter crumbs, which can be fed to one-day-old poults until they are about 4 to 5 weeks old. To encourage poults to start eating you can chop up a hard-boiled egg very finely and mix it in with their crumbs. A chick drinker is the best way to supply water; if you dip their beaks in the water once, this will show them where to drink.

Once the turkeys are almost adult, about 17 to 18 weeks, they can be upgraded to turkey breeder pellets. If you are intending to use them for their meat, you will need finisher or grower pellets, which are specially designed for this purpose.

Feed the pellets early in the morning when it is easy for the bird to digest and will enter the system quickly. An afternoon feed of cereal should be given about two hours before the birds go to roost. Grain stays in the crop for much longer than the pellets, which means the bird will have more sustenance throughout the night. When the weather turns cold, a mixture of corn is warming for the birds.

Like many pets, turkeys love treats. Sunflower seeds not only provide protein but also essential oils, which help condition their feathers. You can also give other titbits, such as fruit, corn on the cob and brassicas, which are ideal for hanging up in the sheds where turkeys go for shelter.

You will need to make sure your feeders and waterers are constantly cleaned to stop the spread of disease. It is an idea to soak them in disinfectant once a week and give them a good scrub, but make sure you rinse them thoroughly with clean water.

BREEDING

If you are new to keeping turkeys and only want to keep a couple, then it is probably not worth trying to breed from them. Poults are difficult to rear in the early stages and quickly succumb to chills if there are any changes in temperature. The easiest way is to buy young poults and them rear them that way. If you are determined to have a go at breeding your own, then it is best to incubate them artificially or use a broody hen. The hen turkey can lay as many as 100 eggs in one breeding season—a period of about five months—but you can force her

into laying by introducing artificial light. A laying bird needs about 14 hours of light each day. A low-wattage bulb over the pen is sufficient and should be started in February, increasing the amount of light by one extra hour a week.

Turkeys can go broody, but they do not make very good mothers. Of course, you may have an exception. If you are lucky and your hen is broody, she will sit on her nest and be impossible to move.

Once you have collected the best specimens for incubation, store them in a cool room, broad end up, for no more than a week before introducing them to the incubator. They need to be at room temperature before putting them in the machine. It is also a good idea to dip them in an egg-sanitizing solution to make sure they are free of disease.

Incubation takes 28 days. After hatching the young poults should be treated the same way as young chicks and kept in a brooder with artificial heat until they are old enough to survive on their own. Make sure they are kept well away from any vermin, and feed them turkey crumbs and water for the first couple of weeks.

GUINEA FOWL

Guinea fowl are relatives of the pheasant and have been bred for food for hundreds of years. They originally came from the Guinea Coast of Africa and for a long time were prized as a rare delicacy, masquerading under the name "Tudor Turkey."

There are many different varieties of guinea fowl, and in some countries they are still hunted in much the same way as the pheasant or the partridge in the United Kingdom. The domesticated birds, which are popular in the United Kingdom, are called helmeted guinea fowl (*numida meleagris*).

They are not difficult to keep, and are quite happy running around with other poultry. It is a good idea to buy your guinea fowl as young birds, otherwise they have a tendency to wander and can become prey to foxes. If they get used to you, they become reasonably tame and seem to be happy to stay close to home, especially if they know that food is always to hand. They do not like being handled, though, and as they are easily agitated will flap and utter loud calls if you dare to get too close. They do, however, act as an early warning system if a rat or bird of prey gets too close, becoming very vocal when they feel threatened.

Because they are quite loud it is not advisable for anyone to keep guinea fowl if they are concerned about their neighbors. However, if you have plenty of space they are good at clearing land of insect pests, especially after a crop has been harvested.

If you have never tasted guinea fowl, the flesh is white and delicate with a distinctive gamey flavor. Guinea fowl are not expensive to keep as they eat a lot of grass and other greenery, so if kept free-range you won't need to provide much extra food.

CHOOSING A BREED

The three most common varieties of guinea fowl are the Pearl, the White and the Lavender. The Pearl, sometimes referred to as Pearl Gray, are dark gray with white dots throughout their plumage. White are pure white with just a few black feathers at the back of the neck. The meat on the white bird is lighter than on the other colors and so is the pigment of the skin. Lavender–light blue with little white dots– is one of the preferred colors with people who keep guinea fowl.

The more exotic colors include Royal Purple, which is a very dark black color with a beautiful purple sheen. The only dotting and barring appears on the area around the flank. This is one of the most elegant of the varieties. Coral Blues have a blue color that gets darker on the neck, breast and back. The Buff and Buff Dundotte are both light tan in color with the latter having white dots throughout its coat. The Slate variety is very rare and seldom seen. It has a beautiful steel color with an irridescent purple-blue around the neck. The Porcelain has a very pale, pastel blue plumage with white dots.

If you are just looking for a few birds around the place, either as watchdogs or to provide the occasional meal, guinea fowl are ideal. If you are keeping them purely for their meat value, then it would be advisable to go for one of the hybrid strains that have been specifically bred for their rapid growing capacity.

HOUSING

A fenced yard is an ideal place to keep guinea fowl, with a chicken house for shelter. If you want to encourage your guinea hens to go broody, then offer them some hiding places inside the shelter. Guinea fowl love to roost in trees, but they should be encouraged to go into a poultry house at night to keep them safe. Guinea fowl are easily panicked and will quickly stampede away from the source of disturbance, which could be something as trivial as the banging of a door. Although training them to go inside might take time,

with perseverance it is possible to get them into a routine.

Guinea fowl prefer to nest outdoors and will rarely use a nest box. If you are allowing them to roam freely, you might find it difficult to locate their eggs as the nests are usually on the ground and well hidden in hedgerows or tall grasses. By keeping them in a run, it is possible to encourage them to lay indoors, but they will stop laying during winter months.

Guinea fowl originate from a hotter climate and consequently love to bask in the sun at every opportunity. They will withstand rain, but like to have some bushes or trees to shelter under if it gets too heavy. Snow makes them nervous and they seem unwilling to actually step on it, so it would probably be best to keep them inside on really wintry days. Make sure your coop is in a place that gets lots of sun and is sheltered from wind. Apart from these

few provisos they seem to cope with colder climates exceptionally well.

FEEDING

Provide one feeder and waterer for every 20 birds. Any feeders that are inside the coop should be the round, suspended type because these discourage perching. Guinea fowl have relatively small crops, which means they need to feed more frequently than other types of poultry. It is therefore advisable to make sure they have constant access to food and water.

Proprietary chick feed is suitable for young guinea fowl, or keets, followed by a normal grower's ration. Be careful when buying broiler food used for chickens: although this can be used for guinea fowl, certain brands have coccidiostat additives, which are toxic to them. Check with your feed supplier before feeding any to your birds.

If you would like to make up your own feed, keets can survive well on a mixture of hard-boiled eggs, breadcrumbs, and biscuit meal moistened with skimmed milk. After about 10 days they can be given a mixture of barley, wheat, meat meal, ground oats, and cooked rice, which is fed in crumb form. From four weeks of age, dry, mixed grain can be added to their diet. You should also supply grit—a fine grit normally used for pigeons, rather than the larger oyster shell grit for poultry.

BREEDING

Guinea fowl do not make good mothers, so if you wish to breed it is advisable to use either a broody hen or an artificial incubator. The incubation period for their eggs is 28 days and you will need to regulate the heat as follows:

Day-olds	95°F
After 3 days	88°F
After 10 days	84°F

Keep reducing the temperature gradually until it is down to 70°F by the twenty-eighth day. After this period they can be kept at a temperature of around 64°F until they are old enough to withstand fluctuations. Keets cannot withstand damp conditions, so you need to make sure everything is kept clean and dry.

Guinea fowl are impossible to sex as young birds, so you will need to wait until they are about nine weeks old to be certain. This is the age they start to call, and because the male and female have very different methods of communication, it is easy to differentiate between the two—male birds produce a single note, while the females have a two-note sound that can be best described as "pot-rack, pot-rack." When the birds are a little older, the males can easily be identified by their larger wattles and the bigger helmets on top of their heads.

QUAIL

Quail are easy birds to tend and the smaller breeds, such as the Japanese quail or Italian Coturnix, are happy to be kept in runs with small houses. Under the right conditions, quails can lay as many as 300 eggs a year and for this reason they are the perfect choice for the small backyard farmer.

Quail are a member of the pheasant family. Because of their size and exquisite eggs, they have become popular as domesticated birds. They were domesticated in Japan as early as the twelfth century, but in those days, they were kept mainly for their quirky song. They weren't really kept for their meat or eggs until the early 1900s.

Quail eggs are almost identical in flavor and nutritional value to chicken eggs. However, because quails are much smaller, they need very little food and are therefore far cheaper to keep. A Japanese quail can start to produce eggs at less than two months old, while the males can be ready for the table at six to eight weeks. Their life expectancy is short—around two to 2 1/2 years—but the hens should lay daily for at least one year of their life. Quail eggs are still considered to be a delicacy and those of the Japanese breed are a mottled brown color, frequently covered with a light blue, chalky type material.

The female Japanese quail is light tan with black speckling on the throat and upper breast. The males have a rusty brown throat and breast feathers, a cloacal gland, and a bulbous structure found on the upper edge of its vent.

If you are looking for a friendly bird, then the male is more likely to be relaxed in human company. Having a male among your hens can also help to reduce the risk of bullying, as it seems to have a calming effect on the flock.

HOUSING

Because quail are proficient flyers, the best way to keep them is in aviary-type conditions. The housing should have wire sides to stop the birds from getting bored and shavings on the ground. It should also be provided with dust baths and nest boxes filled with hay to give the birds some privacy for laying. The nestbox should be a solid box with a small opening for the hens to use and a larger door for collecting eggs and cleaning. It is possible to keep quails in large rabbit hutches or poultry arks, but you need to make sure they have plenty of room because they are prone to boredom.

Quail need protection from cold winter weather and, because they are naturally ground dwellers, they will not walk up a ramp to their houses like chickens. Some people prefer to keep the cages raised off the ground, because this makes cleaning easier. In raised cages, the droppings can fall to the ground below, which has the advantage of removing the risk of quail standing in their own manure and therefore keeping the eggs clean.

You will need to make sure the run is rat-proof, as quail are easy prey.

One thing you will need to be careful of when first placing quail in their run is that they have a tendency to fly straight up. Because they can gain quite a lot of speed on the way up, some birds have been known to break their necks when they hit the top of the cage. If your cages are high enough to allow flight, you will need to make the tops out of canvas or nylon netting, so that it has enough slack to avoid injuring the birds.

If you are keeping males for their meat, they can be placed in an outdoor pen, giving them room to fly and also allowing them to catch insects, which make up a large part of their diet.

FEEDING

Because these birds are so small, food should be available to them 24 hours a day. If you are raising males for meat, they will thrive on a diet rich in carbohydrates. Hens will need laying mash, if you want them to produce a lot of eggs. It is possible to buy proprietary brands for quail, but make sure they have not been treated or medicated if you wish to keep your birds organically. You can supplement the quail's diet with chopped greens and other vegetable scraps.

Males can also be given table scraps, such as stale bread and cakes, to boost their carbohydrate intake. Clean, fresh water must be available at all times, but make sure the waterers are of a suitable size.

BREEDING

Quail will start to lay when they are around 10 to 12 weeks old. The usual mating ratio is one male to three females. They do not make great mothers, and Japanese quail are incapable of going broody and hatching their own eggs. You will need to place the eggs in an incubator; the incubation period is 18 days. Quail will hatch under the same conditions as other chicks, but the difference is they are so small you will have to make sure they have no means of escape. Place pebbles in the chick drinkers to give the birds somewhere to stand, otherwise you risk them drowning.

USING THE EGGS

The popularity of quail eggs has increased considerably since World War II, and they are renowned for their light texture and softly colored yolks. The varied and attractive patterns of spots, speckles, and blotches on the shells is different on each egg. Even the color can vary depending on the type of nest or bedding provided.

Quail eggs can be eaten in a multitude of ways and are a tasty delight for all occasions. Traditionally they were served either pickled or preserved in aspic jelly, although they can also be enjoyed in much the same way as hens' eggs.

HEALTH

Quails are generally hardy, but so little is known about their illnesses you might struggle to find an avian vet who has enough experience to treat your birds when they are not well. Hopefully you should be able to tell the health of your birds from their general appearance. They should have nice, bright eyes and should not be hunched or fluffed up in a corner of the cage. Quails are generally very active birds, so you should quickly pick up on signs of listlessness. They are prone to lice and mites, like all poultry, but keeping their house and bedding clean should minimize this risk. If you notice your birds pecking at themselves or losing their feathers, you can treat them with a small amount of anti-mite powder. Another indication of health is the condition of the vent. This should be moist and white with no lumps or crusty bits.

Recipes

A SELECTION OF RECIPES

Here are a few recipes to sample using eggs and meat from some of the poultry types covered in this book. There is nothing quite like eating a dish made with ingredients that are totally fresh, including a bird that has enjoyed its life to the full.

EGGS BENEDICT

For a truly extravagant breakfast or brunch, Eggs Benedict with its lightly toasted muffins, really crisp bacon, and perfectly poached eggs, truly hits the spot.

Ingredients   Serves 2

For the hollandaise sauce
5 ounces dry white wine
8 ounces white wine vinegar
15 whole black peppercorns
1 banana shallot, roughly chopped
8 ounces unsalted butter
3 egg yolks

For the Eggs Benedict
white wine vinegar
2 very fresh eggs
2 English muffins, sliced in half and
    toasted
4 strips of bacon or pancetta;
    alternatively 4 slices of ham

Method

1. For the hollandaise sauce, place the white wine, white wine vinegar, peppercorns and shallots in a heavy-based saucepan over a high heat.

2. Bring to the boil and reduce the liquid until it is half its original volume. This should take about 15 minutes.

3. While the mixture is reducing, place the butter in a small, heavy-bottomed pan and melt over a low heat. Once melted, skim any foamy bits from the surface with a spoon. Remove the clarified butter from the heat and allow to cool to blood temperature.

4. Place a clean, glass bowl over a pan of simmering water. Make sure the water doesn't touch the bottom of the bowl.

5. Put the egg yolks in the bowl and whisk. Add 1 tablespoon of the vinegar and shallot reduction. Whisk vigorously and constantly for about 5 minutes until the mixture is foamy and starts to thicken.

6. This stage is ready when the mixture falls from the whisk in strands that rest for a couple of seconds on the surface before sinking back into the mixture.

7. Remove the egg mixture from the heat and pour a small amount of the clarified

butter into the egg mixture. Whisk vigorously until the butter is completely blended. Slowly add the remainder of the butter, whisking constantly until it forms a smooth, thick, emulsified sauce. Make sure you work slowly and that the ingredients are all the same temperature, otherwise you risk the sauce splitting.

8. Now grill your bacon or pancetta until it is really crisp.

9. Now it is time to poach the eggs. Fill a tall pan with water, adding three tablespoons of white wine vinegar to every pint. Bring to the boil and make a "whirlpool" in the pan by swirling a slotted spoon in the water. While the water is still moving, carefully crack the eggs into the center of the whirlpool. Poach until the whites are firm but there is still some movement in the yolk.

10. To serve, place half a muffin on each plate. Top with two slices of bacon or pancetta—or, if you prefer, slices of ham—and the other half of the muffin. Carefully remove the poached eggs from the pan with a slotted spoon and place on top of the muffin. Spoon the hollandaise sauce over the top and around the muffins and serve immediately.

POT-ROASTED QUAIL WITH PANCETTA

This delicious one-pot meal is perfect if you are catering for a large number of people on a chilly night—perfect for winter outdoor celebrations or a rustic post-Christmas treat.

Ingredients Serves 4

4 fresh quail
8 sage leaves
8 thin slices of pancetta (or as much as needed to cover birds)
1 tbsp olive oil
1 tbsp butter
1 onion, finely diced
2 carrots, finely diced
4 celery stalks, finely diced
2 bay leaves
Sea salt and pepper
5 ounces dry white wine
5 ounces chicken stock
1 tbsp butter
Few sprigs thyme

Method

1. Wipe each quail inside and out with a piece of damp kitchen paper. Place a couple of sage leaves inside each bird and then wrap with the pancetta.

2. Heat the olive oil and butter in a large frying pan. When sizzling, add the onion, carrot, bay leaves, celery, salt, and pepper and cook until soft, stirring occasionally.

3. Transfer the vegetables to a large, heatproof casserole with a lid. Add the wine and stock and then place on the heat for a minute or two until it starts to bubble.

4. Add a little extra oil and butter to the frying pan and brown the quails on both sides, then arrange on top of the vegetables in the casserole dish.

5. Put the lid on the casserole, reduce the heat to very low, and simmer for about 30 to 40 minutes, or until the legs are easy to remove.

6. Once cooked, portion the quails into easy-to-eat pieces. Add the butter and thyme to the vegetables left in the casserole, stir, and then serve with the pieces of quail on top.

This dish is wonderful served with some creamy mashed potato, or simply eaten with a warm, rustic loaf of bread.

GUINEA FOWL WITH GARLIC AND ROSEMARY

If you are looking for a great alternative to chicken or turkey, then guinea fowl is worth considering with its subtle gamey flavor. It can be simply roasted as you would any other fowl, or combined with more robust flavors as in the following recipe.

Ingredients   Serves 4

1 guinea fowl, cut into chunks
plain flour for dusting, seasoned with salt and freshly ground black pepper
5 ounces extra virgin olive oil
4 garlic cloves, sliced lengthways
large bunch rosemary, broken in half
5 ounces white wine

Method

1. Toss the guinea fowl in the seasoned flour.

2. Heat the olive oil in a large, heavy-based frying pan. When hot, add the guinea fowl and seal well on all sides, until golden brown and quite crispy.

3. Reduce the heat to low, add the garlic and rosemary and cover the pan with a lid. Cook for 30 minutes, turning the meat from time to time.

4. After 30 minutes, increase the heat to high and remove the lid. Add the white wine and allow it to reduce to half its original volume.

5. To serve, toast some bruschetta and rub with garlic. Drizzle over some olive oil from the guinea fowl sauce and serve with the guinea fowl on top.

GLAZED DUCK WITH SAUTEED PARSNIPS

Slightly sweet parsnips complement the richness of the duck in this recipe. The delicious fruity glaze is easy to make. Serve with green beans and warmed French bread.

Ingredients   Serves 4
1 cup small parsnips, peeled and cut into 1/4" slices
2 onions, each cut into 8 wedges
4 duck breast fillets, about 6 ounces each
1 tbsp sunflower oil
8 tbsp brandy
4 tbsp blackcurrant cordial (at least 50 percent fruit squash)
juice of 1 lemon
parsley sprigs, to garnish

Method
1. Put the parsnips and onions into a large saucepan with water and bring to the boil. Simmer for 5 minutes until the parsnips are tender but still firm. Drain thoroughly, then return the vegetables to the pan.

2. While the vegetables are cooking, prick the skin of the duck all over without cutting into the meat. Heat the oil in a large frying pan over high heat and then add the duck breasts with the skin side facing down. Reduce the heat and cook, pressing down on the duck from time to time, but do not turn the pieces over. Cook until the skin is crisp and really brown and the fat is starting to run out.

3. Drizzle some of the duck fat over the parnips and onions and mix well. Put on a low to medium heat to brown lightly while the duck finishes cooking. Stir and turn the parsnips and onions occasionally, adding seasoning to taste. Make sure the vegetables do not overcook, the parsnips should remain firm. Transfer to warm plates.

4. Pour off the remaining fat from the frying pan containing the duck and turn the breasts over. Cook them over a low to medium heat for another 10 to 15 minutes. They should be cooked through but still remain slightly pink in the middle. Season to taste and arrange over the vegetables. If you prefer you can slice the meat at this stage.

5. To make the glaze. Add the brandy and blackcurrant cordial to the frying pan. Bring to the boil over a high heat and boil for 30 seconds, stirring in the sediment from the pan. Reduce the mixture to a sticky, aromatic sauce and pour over the duck.

GLOSSARY

This section provides definitions of most of the terms that you are likely to come across in the world of keeping poultry. Please note the terms relating to health and disease can be found on pages 80 to 92.

Abdomen—The area under the body from the breast to the stern.

Abcess—A pocket filled with pus.

Addled eggs—Fertile eggs that die soon after the start of incubation.

Air cell—The area containing oxygen at the wide end of the egg.

Albumen—The white protein area of the egg.

Alektorophobia—The fear of chickens.

Alimentary tract—The specialized tube that runs from the mouth to the vent, where digestion and egestion take place.

Allantois—A sac connected to the embryo's abdomen that allows the embryo to breathe. It also stores excretions and absorbs albumen used for food by the embryo.

Amino acids—Digested proteins ready for absorption into the bloodstream.

Amnion—A transparent sac filled with colorless fluid that surrounds the embryo.

Anaemia—A deficiency of the blood is characterized by weakness or pale skin.

Antibiotics—Medication for fighting bacterial infections, given internally.

Antibodies—Miscroscopic agents formed in bone marrow and spleen and circulated in the blood as a defense against viral disease.

Ark—Type of movable poultry house with a slatted floor. Traditionally used for growers.

Artificial insemination (AI)—The collection of semen from the male, followed by its injection via a syringe into the vent and oviduct of the female.

Ash—The mineral component of feed.

Atrophy—A shrinking or wasting away of a body part.

Avian—Relating to the characteristics of birds; or derived from birds.

Autosexing breed—One that produces readily identifiable sexes at hatching because of the barring on the plumage.

Aviculture—The science of raising avian species.

Axial feather—Small feather between the primary and secondary feathers of the wing.

Baffle—Board used in a poultry house in conjunction with an air vent. Prevents down-draft without restricting ventilation.

Ballooning—Distension of the intestine or caeca due to accumulated blood or mucus.

Bantam—Small-sized fowl, either true bantam or miniaturized versions of the larger breeds.

Barnyard chicken—A chicken of mixed breed.

Barring—Where stripes or another color run across the feathers. Openly-barred is stripes that are far apart and of a different color. Also refers to the sex-linked barring gene.

Battery system—An intensive system of egg production where layers are kept in cages in environmentally controlled houses.

Beak—Horny projection consisting of upper and lower mandibles, forming the mouth parts; otherwise known as the bill.

Beak trimming—Removal of the tip of the upper beak to stop pecking and cannibalism.

Bean—A hard protuberance on the upper mandible of waterfowl.

Beard—A tuft of feathers underneath the beak in certain breeds.

Bedding—Material scattered on the floor of a coop or poultry house to absorb moisture and manure.

Blade—The lower, undivided part of a single comb.

Blastoderm—A fertilized true egg.

Bleaching—The fading of color from the beak, vent and shanks of a yellow-skinned laying hen.

Blood spot—A tiny red spot in a freshly laid egg.

Bloom—The protective coating on a freshly laid egg.

Blowout—Damage to the vent caused by laying an oversized egg.

Booted—Having feathers on the shanks and toes.

Breast—Area of the body from the neck to the central part of the body between the legs.

Breed—A group of birds with similar appearance and characteristics, having a distinctive body and features that are reproduced when mated.

Broiler—Fowl bred and raised for the table.

Brood—To care for a batch of chicks, or the chicks themselves.

Brooder—A protected area with artificial heat for raising chicks.

Brooding period—The time between when the chicks are hatched until they can survive on their own.

Broodiness—The maternal instinct in a female to want to sit on and incubate a clutch of eggs.

Bursa of Fabricius—Cloacal bursa.

Candling—To examine the contents of an egg using light.

Cannibalism—The habit of chickens eating each others' flesh, feathers or eggs.

Cape—The feathers between the shoulders and under the hackles.

Capon—A castrated male fowl that has been neutered to increase growth rate.

Carbohydrates—Heat and energy producing foods found in grains and vegetables.

Cecum (*pl. ceca*)—A pouch where the small and large intestine meet.

Carriage—The way in which a bird holds itself and walks.

Cephalic—Pertaining to the head or skull.

Chalazae—Internal membranes in the white of an egg, that keep the yolk suspended in the middle.

Calcar—The bone protruding from a mature male bird's shank.

Chick—A young bird of either sex, up to the age of six weeks.

Chick crumbs—Proprietary feed or starter ration formulated for chicks.

Chick tooth—A tiny, sharp, horny projection at the end of the chick's upper beak used to break out of the shell.

Clavicle—Wishbone.

Clean-legged—Having no feathers growing down the shanks.

Clears—Eggs that are found to be infertile on candling.

Cloaca—The opening at the end of the rectum.

Close feathering—Where feathers are held close to the body.

Clubbed down—Down that fails to emerge in an embryo or newly hatched chick.

Cluck—The sound a hen makes to comfort her chicks.

Clutch—The number of eggs laid by one hen.

Cock—Male bird over the age of 12 months; also called a rooster.

Cockerel—A male chicken under one year of age.

Cock fighting—A sport using game birds to fight each other, which is illegal in many parts of the world.

Colony house—Moveable house on wheels for a small flock.

Comb—The fleshy growth on top of the head.

Condition— The general state of a bird in relation to its health, cleanliness and appearance.

Coop—Small house in which a chicken lives.

Corn—A grain constituent of poultry feed.

Coverts—Tail coverts are the small feathers at the base of the tail. Wing coverts are those covering the tops of the flight feathers.

Crest—Tuft of feathers on the top of the head.

Crop—Area of the lower gullet where food is stored before passing into the gizzard for further digestion.

Cross breeding—The mating of two birds of different breeds.

Crow-headed—A serious defect in show birds, also an indicator of a poor layer.

Cuckoo—Feather markings similar to barring.

Culling—Disposing of unsuitable birds from a flock.

Culture—To incubate a sample from a diseased bird.

Cushion—The soft feathers on a hen's rump.

Cuticle—The protective bloom left on a new laid egg as it dries.

Dam—A female parent.

Day-olds—Newly hatched chicks.

Dead-in-shell—Chick embryos that began to develop in the shell but died before hatching.

De-beak—To remove a portion of a bird's top beak to prevent feather pulling or cannibalism.

Deep litter—A system of housing on litter such as wood shavings.

Defect—Any aspect that detracts from perfection in the standards of show birds.

Depopulate—To get rid of an entire flock.

Dewlap—The single flap of skin below the beak of turkeys and certain geese.

Dominant—Genetic characteristic that appears in the progeny of a first hybridized cross.

Down—Soft feather covering of the newly hatched chick.

Drake—Male duck.

Drawing—Eviscerating or gutting a chicken.

Droppings—Bird manure.

Drumstick—Tibia or lower thigh, as referred to in a meat bird.

Dual-purpose breed—A utility bird that is both a good layer and also suitable for the table.

Dub—To surgically remove a bird's comb and wattles close to the head.

Duckling—A young duck.

Dust bath—An area of fine soil that the bird allows to trickle through its feathers to get rid of parasites.

Earlobes—The fleshy part of bare skin below the ears.

Ectoparasites—External parasites such as mites and ticks.

Egg—The female germ cell.

Egg-grading—A system of quality checks for eggs being sold for human consumption.

Egg sanitant—An antiseptic solution for ensuring that hatching eggs are free of external pathogens.

Egg sizes—Sizes that are recognized for the purposes of labelling and selling.

Embryo—The developing chick within the egg.

Embryology—The study of the development of embryos.

Endoparasites—Internal parasites such as worms and coccidia.

Face—The area around and below the eyes where no feathers grow.

Fancier—One who breeds birds for exhibition.

Feather-legged—Having feathers growing down the shanks.

Feed conversion ratio (FCR)—Ratio of food eaten in relation to weight or number of eggs produced.

Fiber—The indigestible element of food that enables the bowels to work efficiently.

First-cross—The progeny of two different breeds mated together.

Flights—The long feathers of the wings (also called primaries).

Flock—A group of chickens living together.

Fluff—Soft feathers on abdomen and thighs.

Fold unit—Moveable house on grass.

Fowl—General term for domesticated birds.

Free-range—A system of keeping birds that are not confined.

Frizzle—Feathers that curl rather than lay flat.

Gallus domesticus—The domestic chicken.
Gallus Gallus—The Red Jungle fowl.
Gall bladder—Small organ producing secretions for the digestive system.
Gamebirds—Any of several species including Pheasant, Quail, and Partridge that are traditionally hunted for food.
Gander—Male goose.
Gapes—The action of a bird in opening and closing its beak in a gasping action.
Genotype—The genetic makeup of a bird.
Gizzard—The true stomach of a bird.
Goose—A female goose.
Gosling—A young goose of either sex.
Grit—Solid mineral particles that aid digestion.
Grower—A young bird between 6 weeks and maturity.
Grower ration—Compound feed formulated for the needs of growing birds.
Guinea fowl—A pheasant-like bird.
Gullet—The tubular structure leading from the mouth to the stomach.

Hackles—Long, narrow neck feathers.
Handling—The art of picking up and handling a bird without causing stress.
Hangers—Thin feathers that hang down at the root of the male's tail.
Hard feathering—Tight, close feathering.
Hardening off—The period when young birds no longer have artificial heat, but are not yet ready to go outside.

Hatching—The emergence of the chick from its shell.
Haugh unit—Measurement of the height of the egg white, as used to denote freshness.
Heavy breed—Large breed or sitter with a greater tendency to become broody.
Hen—Female bird over 12 months.
Hock—The joint between the lower thigh and shank.
Hopper—Feeder made of two parts.
Hover—A heated canopy or roof for brooding chicks.
Humidity—The amount of moisture in the air.
Hybrid—Progeny produced by breeding from two or more distinct lines.

Impaction—The blockage of a body passage or cavity such as the crop or cloaca.
In-breeding—Mating birds that are related to each other.
Incubation—The process of development of an embryo in the shell.
Incubator—An artificially heated container for hatching eggs.
Infertile—An egg that is not fertilized and will not hatch.

Joule—Unit of measurement of energy levels in feeds.
Jejunum—Middle small intestine.

Keel—The breast bone to which the flying muscles of the wings are attached.
Keet—A guinea fowl chick.

Kibbling—Chopping up grain into smaller particles, as distinct from grinding it.

Knee—Joint between the upper and lower thighs.

Laceration—Jagged wound.

Lacing—Pattern on the plumage where the outside edge of a feather is a different color or shade from the rest.

Layer—Mature female chicken kept for egg production.

Layer ration—Any prepared feed containing all the necessary nutrients for a layer to produce good quality eggs.

Leader—Tapering spike or end point at the rear of the rose comb.

Leaf comb—A comb resembling a broad leaf.

Leaker—An egg that leaks because the shell and membrane are both broken.

Leg—Area consisting of upper and lower thigh and shank.

Leg feathering—Where feathers are found instead of the usual scales.

Light breed—Lighter in weight than a heavy breed, with less tendency to become broody.

Litter—General term for ground covering.

Mandible—The lower, moveable part of the beak.

Marbling—Spotted pattern on the feathers.

Mash— Compound feed of grains and other food materials.

Mealy-feathered—A fault in a show bird where brown or buff feathers are spotted with white.

Meat breeds—Breeds kept specifically for the table because of their quick growth and heavy muscles.

Meat spot—Tiny white, gray or brown speck in a freshly-laid egg.

Molting—The annual process of losing old feathers and growing new ones.

Mossy-feathered—White feathers spotted with brown.

Mottling—White tipping on the ends of feathers.

Muff—Feathering on each side of the face.

Natural brooding—Where chicks are protected by a mother hen rather than being raised in an artificial incubator.

Nest—A secluded place where a hen lays her eggs.

Nostrils—Openings at the base of the upper beak for respiration.

Oats—Grain used in feeds.

Oesophagus—Gullet or area of the digestive system from the mouth to crop.

Out-breeding—Mating different strains of the same breed.

Oviduct—Passage from the ovary to the vent down which the egg travels.

Oyster shell—Crushed shell that provides a source of calcium.

Papilla—The projection on the shank of a bird that eventually develops into a spur in male birds.

Parson's nose—The uropygium, a bony and fleshy protruberance from which the tail feathers grow.

Pasting—Loose droppings sticking to the vent area.

Pathogen—An organism that causes disease.

Pea comb—A small, low, triple comb.

Pecking order—The social rank of chickens.

Pencilling—Line markings on the feathers.

Perch—The place where a chicken sleeps at night, also called a roost.

Pin feathers—The tips of newly emerging feathers.

Pipping—Where a hatching chick breaks a hole in the eggshell.

Pituitary gland—Small gland in the brain that controls the egg-laying mechanism.

Plumage—Total set of feathers covering birds.

Point-of-lay (POL)—The period from 18 to 21 weeks when a pullet is about to lay for the first time.

Popeye—Emaciation of chicks, causing eyes to look large in relation to body.

Pop hole—A poultry house exit.

Pot egg—A pottery egg placed in a nest to encourage hens to lay.

Poussin—A table bird killed at an early stage for a specialist market.

Precocity—Starting to lay before growth is complete.

Proventriculus—The glandular stomach area before the gizzard.

Pullet—A female chicken under one year of age.

Purebred—The offspring of purebred parents that are of the same class, breed and variety.

Rales—Any abnormal sounds coming from the airways.

Range fed—Description of chickens that are allowed to range pasture.

Roost—The place where the chicken sleeps at night.

Rooster—A male chicken over one year old.

Rooster egg—A very small egg containing no yolk, also called a wind egg.

Saddle—The part of a chicken's back just before the tail.

Saddle feathers—"Sex feathers" on a chicken's saddle.

Scales—The small, hard overlapping plates on a chicken's shanks and toes.

Scratcher—An affectionate name given to a free-range chicken.

Secondaries—Inner quill feather of the wings.

Self color—Single plumage color.

Serrations—Divisions of the comb.

Setting—Fertile eggs that are being stored before incubation.

Sex link—Any inherited factor linked to the sex chromosomes of either parent.

Shank—Area of the leg between the foot and the hock joint.

Sheen—Gloss on the plumage.

Shell—Hard outer surface of an egg.

Sickles—Long, curved tail feathers.

Single comb—Narrow, thin comb surmounted by serrations.

Sire—Male parent.

Sitting—Fertile eggs sold for incubation, or a number of eggs that one hen can cover.

Snood—Fleshy appendage on the face of a turkey that hangs down alongside the beak.

Spangling—Spots of splashes of different colors on the feathers.

Split comb—A division in the blade of a single comb.

Split crest—The division of the crest.

Split tail—A gap in the base of the main tail feathers.

Spraddle legs—An affliction that prevents a chick from standing upright.

Spur—The horny growth on the shank of the male, used in fighting.

Strain—A number of birds from the same family group of one breed.

Striping—Dark line down the center of a white feather.

Stubs—Sheaths of small quill feathers left behind on plucking.

Supplements—Minerals and vitamins added to feed.

Thighs—Muscles covering area above the shank, always covered with feathers.

Throat—The upper and front area of the neck.

Tibia—See Drumstick.

Ticking—Small dark dots on feathers.

Tipping—The tips of feathers are a different color or shade from the rest.

Trap-nest—A nest designed to automatically close behind a hen so that an egg can be identified as hers before she is released.

Tom—A male turkey.

Treading—Mating, as described by the action of the cock's feet on the back of the hen.

Tri-colored—A breed with the neck hackle, saddle hackle and wing bows of different colors.

Trio—A group of one male and two females.

Trussing—Preparing a bird for the oven.

Turkey—A large game bird.

Uropygium—See Parson's nose.

Utility chickens—Ones bred for productive purposes rather than showing.

Variety—A subdivision of a breed, distinguished by color and other features.

Vent—Opening of the oviduct from which the egg emerges.

Ventriculus—The gizzard.

Vitelline membrane—Thin membrane that encloses the ovum.

Vulture hock—Stiff feathers growing out from the hock joint.

Walnut comb—A type of comb also referred to as the strawberry comb.

Waterglass—Sodium silicate solution, traditionally used for storing eggs.

Wattles—Fleshy lobes suspended from the jaw.

Weathering—A yellow or brassy tint in white feathered birds.

Web—The skin between the toes or between the joints in the wings.

Wheat—Feed grain.

Wind egg—A small egg containing no yolk.

Wing bay—Secondary wing feathers that form a triangular pattern when the wing is folded.

Wing clipping—The annual practice of clipping the ends of primary feathers on one wing to stop a bird from flying away.

Wings—The fore-limbs.

Wry tail—A congenital deformity in which the tail is twisted to one side.

Xanthophylls—a pigment found in leaves, grasses, and green plants, that results in darker egg yolks if ingested by poultry.

Yolk—Ovum, the round yellow mass that provides nourishment to the developing embryo.

Yolk sac—The follicle where an ovum and its surrounding yolk are held until the yolk matures and is released.

Zoning—Laws regulating or restricting the use of land for a particular purpose, such as raising chickens.

Zoonosis—Diseases that can be transmitted from poultry to humans.

INDEX